Marketing and Communication in Higher Education

This series seeks to critically address marketing and communication related issues in higher education. The series aims to be broad in scope (any aspect of higher education that broadly connects with markets, marketization, marketing and communication) and specific in its rationale to provide critical perspectives on higher education with the aim of improving higher education's emancipatory potential.

Albert N. Greco

The College Textbook Publishing Industry in the U.S. 2000–2022

The Search for Competitive Marketing Strategies

Albert N. Greco
Gabelli School of Business
Fordham University
Bronx, NY, USA

Marketing and Communication in Higher Education
ISBN 978-3-031-30414-9   ISBN 978-3-031-30415-6   (eBook)
https://doi.org/10.1007/978-3-031-30415-6

This Palgrave Macmillan imprint is published by the registered company Springer Nature Switzerland AG.
The registered company address is: Gewerbestrasse 11, 6330 Cham, Switzerland

For Elaine

PREFACE

Merriam Webster's Collegiate Dictionary defines the word textbook as "a book used in the study of a subject; as (a): one containing a presentation of the principles of a subject; (b): a literary work relevant to the study of a subject."[1] This means that any required book for a college, graduate, or professional school class is considered a "textbook" in a U.S. college or independent bookstore or on the diverse online websites. So, a "textbook" can be a "traditional" large hard cover book used in an introductory physics class, or it can be a trade hard bound or paperback book used in an introductory history class or a hard bound or paperback university press or a scholarly professional book used in a business or law school class.

Exceptionally important statistical data about the college sector is collected and analyzed about college textbooks (also known as higher education textbooks; in this book "college textbooks" or "higher education textbooks" will be used interchangeably) by a number of important and reliable sources, including The U.S. Department of Commerce (Commerce), Bureau of the Census (Census); the U.S. Department of Labor (Labor), Bureau of Labor Statistics (BLS); the U.S. Department of Education (Education), the National Center for Education Statistics (NCES); the Association of American Publishers (AAP); Nielsen; *The Statistical Abstract of the United States; The Bowker Annual* (the name of this important annual book series was changed in 2008 to *The Library and Book Trade Almanac*); and the National Association of College Stores (NACS). Many of these sources collect, aggregate, and release data on a monthly, a quarterly, or an annual basis about college textbooks.

Several of these organizations (e.g., Education; Commerce; AAP; etc.) also release data on the other major book categories including trade books (i.e., adult, juvenile and children's, mass market, and religion), educational textbooks and educational materials (e.g., K-12), professional books (i.e., scientific, technical, and medical books, also called STM), and university press books. Clearly, ascertaining the percentage of these book categories that are adopted for college student use would be impossible to determine since the various U.S. governmental departments and other reliable sources of data do not reveal detailed information about college adoption revenues for trade, K-12, professional, or university presses. So, while hardcover or paperback trade, professional, and university press books are required in certain academic disciplines (e.g., the humanities; the social sciences; the diverse legal, tax, and regulatory areas; and the scientific, technical, and medical fields), trade, K-12, professional, and university press book revenues and unit sales will be excluded in this book.

In the U.S., the word "college" or "university" refers to a private or public two-year community or junior college or a four-year college (e.g., The College of New Jersey). Graduate school refers to a university, an institution of higher education, which offers graduate degrees (e.g., the Ph.D., Stanford University). A professional school is a higher education institution, which offers a professional degree (e.g., M.D., The University of Kansas). So, the words textbooks, higher education textbooks, or college textbooks will be used interchangeably. In addition, all numbers were rounded off and may not always equal 100%. In addition, all college textbook revenues in this book are net publisher revenues or net publisher units (i.e., gross sales minus returns equals net revenues or net units). Lastly, colleges in the U.S. use academic years (e.g., 2000–2001); however, a single year, for example, 2000, will refer to an academic year unless otherwise noted.

In 2000, the five largest textbook publishers in the U.S. (often called the "Big 5") included Pearson PLC (also known as Pearson or Prentice Hall), Cengage Learning, McGraw-Hill, John Wiley, and Macmillan Academic. These five companies had a combined annual market share of approximately 80% generating collectively billions of dollars annually. However, many of these publishers also published trade books and products in various non-higher education sectors. For example, for decades Pearson was a major trade book publisher (e.g., The Penguin Classics).

John Wiley was a large scholarly journal and professional book publisher with a trade book line (they published the famous and ubiquitous *Dummies* books). There were a number of "smaller" publishers active in the higher education space (e.g., W.W. Norton).

Overall, the "Big 5" publishing houses looked at the higher education sector, in 2000, with pride and pleasure. After all, they were part of the pivotal cultural industry of the nation. They published substantive texts that transmitted ideas, knowledge, and important intellectual content. Their books contained theories (e.g., physics or chemistry textbooks) as well as practical information (e.g., accounting auditing procedures). Their titles enabled students to read about the Romantic poetry of Bryon, Shelley, Keats, Wordsworth, and Coleridge, and they provided detailed and illustrative information about the rigid structure of medieval French society where the aristocracy ruled pivotal institutions. Publishers believed their texts were important in understanding the history of a nation and the world, and they published books that conveyed "must have, need to know" information (e.g., for nursing school students). In addition, enrollments were growing at a rapid pace as were publisher's sales, revenues, units, and profits, so they believed that this industry was in very good shape for the foreseeable future.

What they failed to understand were the underlying concerns, unhappiness, and, at times growing hostility about how students and some faculty members viewed the textbook sector's frequent textbook revisions and the steep pricing strategies for printed textbooks.

This book explores the college textbook publishing industry, from its inception in medieval universities, through the late twentieth century, to the present day which has led to an existential crisis for some publishers. The various sections in this book offer a comprehensive analysis of the substantive developments, problems, and concerns about a myriad of major issues that confronted the higher education textbook sector after 2000.

Chapter 1 provides an overview of the development of textbooks in Europe and then this section provides coverage of U.S. textbook developments to 2000. Chapter 2 addresses the impact of disruption technologies during the years 2001–2012 (e.g., online websites selling used and rental textbooks), changes in college enrollments, and various U.S. recessions (e.g., a brief economic downturn in 2001 and a deep recession in

2007–2009). These developments upended what had been a highly successful and lucrative industry dependent on a steady stream of the sale of new textbooks in independent and chain college bookstores to students. Chapter 3 reviews the years (2013–2018) of the important legal and copyright challenges and threats to traditional textbook sales ranging from copyright infringement issues, the importation of textbooks printed legally in foreign jurisdictions (e.g., Thailand) and whether these texts could be imported legally into the U.S., the growing concerns about textbook piracy, the attempt to create a secondary market for the re-sale of used digital products (including digital e-textbooks), and the launch of an innovative, yet controversial, "inclusive access" (i.e., IA) textbook sales strategy.

Chapter 4 analyzes the effective and, at times, ineffective strategies launched by U.S. textbook publishers between 2019 and 2021 to address the direct threats to their basic business models. The final Chap. 5 offers comments and observations about the future of this important yet threatened industry.

This book also incorporated, into the various sections, highly reliable textbook statistical sources as well as a review of some marketing theories utilized by these publishers (e.g., understanding the threat of substitute products, the sale of used and rental texts, the sale of new digital textbooks). This was done to provide an understanding of the state of this industry.

Lastly, based on several decades analyzing this industry, the overarching theses presented in this book about the U.S. textbook industry were as follows. First, textbook publishing was almost from its founding in colonial America a complex business publishing titles (e.g., biology) in a broad number of academic fields (e.g., science, technology, engineering, and medical areas; often called STM or STEM). Second, textbook publishing faced the constant threat of a "substitute" product(s), which included used or a rental copy rather than a new copy of a textbook. Third, these publishers were reliant on their "suppliers," including the financial demands of major authors (i.e., academic "stars") who commanded large advances and high royalty rates. Fourth, textbook publishing was a "fluid and adaptative" business that published books as new academic fields emerged (e.g., ethnic studies, gender studies). Fifth, college textbook publishing was an industry with intense competition among the "Big 5" firms and the smaller textbook publishers to gain market share and revenues. Sixth, there was a threat of "new entrants" entering the textbook sector, especially the open access and self-publishing movement and the ubiquitous online operations, offering inexpensive used and rental printed book and digital textbooks. This meant there was a never-ending quest by the publishers: to create a competitive advantage (known as a "unique value proposition" to economists) and to "get big" and achieve scale and economics of mass production (sometimes relying on a merger or acquisition to achieve this goal).

Seventh, the "Big 5" publishers were committed to moving away from a primarily printed textbook environment to a hybrid (i.e., offering both printed and digital textbooks), and finally to an entirely digital e-textbook world (digital textbooks and e-textbooks are used interchangeably in this book). The goals were to increase profit margins, combat the growing influence of the online used and rental textbooks, and the insidious impact of piracy and copyright infringement. Eight, all of the textbook publishers were concerned about the power of "customers" (i.e., faculty members) to adopt a textbook for class use; the student who purchased the textbook was viewed as the "end user." Ninth, these publishers started to move rapidly toward what economists call "disintermediation," that is, selling or renting printed or digital textbooks directly to students and bypassing sales to traditional college bookstores. The goal was to reclaim the discount offered to college bookstores (averaging about 23 percent) of a textbook's suggested retail price (SRP). Tenth, college textbook publishing was a business where about 20% of a publisher's textbook catalogue titles generated about 80% of a firm's revenues. So, this meant that a publisher needed "big" textbooks written by major (star) authors capable of selling +100,000 copies (known as "units" in the business) to cover the smaller revenues generated by titles selling in the 10,000 to 20,000 unit range; this "80–20" phenomenon is known as the "Pareto Power Law."

All of the college textbook publishers knew they had to create viable business competitive strategies (e.g., a best-selling textbook) and the necessary structures (e.g., printed and digital textbooks; learning management systems, called LMSs; ancillary products for faculty members, perhaps standardized test questions, power point slides, chapter outlines, etc.) to achieve their goals of scale, market share, and profits. What haunted the publishers was the fear that a number of carefully crafted competitive strategies and structural elements often failed in the rugged, often fickle college textbook marketspace. So, what follows is an analysis of the college textbook business for the years 2000 to 2022 and some material about 2023, listing the successes and failures, of what is a pivotal component in the intellectual, cultural, and business life of the U.S. and academia.

New Jersey, USA   Albert N. Greco
January 15, 2023

NOTE

1. *Merriman-Webster's Collegiate Dictionary 10th ed.,* (Springfield, MA: Merriam-Webster, Inc., 1993), p. 1220.

ACKNOWLEDGMENTS

I thank Milana Vernikova for the interest and support toward this book and the superb staff at Palgrave Macmillan in the U.S. and especially abroad for their impressive assistance in the development and publication of this book. I also thank Marcus Ballenger for his early interest in this book and Robert Baensch, the editor of *Publishing Research Quarterly* (PRQ), for his interest in my research.

DISCLAIMER

A large number of companies were mentioned in this book. However, my wife and I do not own stock in any company. All of our financial assets are handled exclusively by T.I.A.A. where I have no say in buys and sells.

Abstract

Since the colonial period, undergraduate, graduate, and professional school students in the U.S. in a variety of academic fields relied on printed textbooks and educational materials to understand complex scientific theories, historical developments, philosophical ideas, and so on. The college (also called higher education) textbook publisher's basic business model worked for centuries; books were published; students purchased textbooks mainly in college or independent bookstores; and publishers earned a steady return on invested capital (ROIC). In 2000, the sale of new college textbooks generated $3.24 billion in net publishers' revenues (Association of American Publishing data [AAP]). However, starting in the late 1990s, and accelerating after 2000, technological disruption undermined the basic business model: used and rental textbooks were readily available on online websites; piracy and copyright infringements threats emerged; Open Educational Resources (OER), Open Access (OA) textbooks, and self-published textbooks became popular. Many college professors used case studies, articles, and lecture materials, and publishers' new textbook revenues increased rather modestly to $3.26 billion in 2021 (+0.62%). This book explores the college textbook publishing industry, from its inception in medieval universities, through the late twentieth century, to the present day which has led to an existential crisis for some publishers. In addition, this study analyzes the substantive changes the industry confronted, and the different managerial, marketing (e.g., Inclusive Access; IA), technology (i.e., CD-ROMs; Learning Management Systems, LMS;

e-textbooks), economic, and financial strategies crafted by college textbook publishers since 2000 to identify, understand, cope with, and minimize or defeat threats to their business model. The book also presents some projections, detailed statistical data, and an extensive bibliography.

Keywords College textbooks • Higher education • Strategy • Disruption • Publishing

CONTENTS

About the Author

Albert N. Greco is Professor of Marketing at Fordham University's Gabelli School of Business in New York City.

His research was cited in the Supreme Court of the United States majority decision by Justice Breyer (Kirtsaeng DBA BlueChristine 99 v. John Wiley & Sons. Inc.; March 19, 2013, decision of the Court) and in three Harvard Business School cases ("Random House" and "Grand Central Publishing," both versions).

He is the author or editor of 18 scholarly books and 10 professional books, including *The Business of Scholarly Publishing: Managing in Turbulent Times* (2020); *The Marketing of World War II: A Business History of the U.S. Government and the Media and Entertainment Industries* (Cham, Switzerland: Palgrave Macmillan; 2020); *The Growth of Scholarly Publishing in the U.S.: A Business History of a Changing Marketplace, 1939–1946* (Cham, Switzerland: Palgrave Macmillan, 2020); *The Economics of the Publishing and the Information Industries: The Search for Yield in a Disintermediated World* (2015); and *The Book Publishing Industry, 3rd edition* (2014).

He is the author of 112 book reviews (in *Publishers Weekly*), 25 book chapters that appeared in *The Oxford Handbook of Publishing; The Oxford Companion to the Book; The Library and Book Trade Almanac 2015: 60th Edition; The Encyclopedia of Library and Information Science; International Book Publishing: An Encyclopedia*, and so on; 59 business articles; and author or co-author of 36 scholarly journal articles (in *Learned Publishing,* and many in *Publishing Research Quarterly,* a Springer Nature journal).

His research papers have been presented at Harvard University, University of Pennsylvania-Wharton School, Oxford University, Cambridge University, The Library of Congress, Catholic University of America, The World Bank, The University of Toronto, The Academy of Marketing Science, The National Endowment for the Arts, The National Geographic Society, INFORMS Market Science, The Society for Scholarly Publishing, George Washington University, and so on.

He was the series editor for the "Allyn & Bacon Series in Mass Communications." He was a senior advisor to the *Journal of Advertising Research.* He serves on the editorial boards of two scholarly journals.

His research has been cited in scholarly journals (including): *American Sociological Review; Canadian Journal of Sociology; The Canadian Review of American Studies; Cardozo Law Review; Enterprise & Society; International Journal of Economics, Finance, and Management Sciences; Journal of the Australian Library and Information Association; Journal of Cultural Economics; Journal of Industrial Economics; Journal of Information Science; Journal of Management Information Systems; Journal of Management Studies; Journal of Marketing; Management Science; PloS One; Quantitative Marketing and Economics; Scientometrics; Vanderbilt Law Review;* scholarly books published by (including) Cambridge University Press, MIT Press, Oxford University Press, Princeton University Press, University of California Press, Singapore University Press, University of Chicago Press, University of Pennsylvania Press, and in Ph.D. dissertations: Erasmus University, Rotterdam; Leiden University; Nanyang Technological University, Singapore; Royal Melbourne Institute of Technology, Australia; University of Maryland; University of Michigan; The University of St. Gallan, Graduate School of Business Administration, Economics, Law, and Social Sciences; University of Southern California; University of Toronto's Joseph L. Rothman School of Management; *Universitat* Tubinger; and so on.

He has appeared on CNBC, PBS, NPR, and the Market Watch Radio Network. He has been interviewed and/or his research cited in *The New York Times; The Wall Street Journal;* Credit Suisse; *The Financial Times; The Washington Post; The Los Angeles Times; The Chicago Tribune; The Denver Post; The Chicago Sun-Times; The Philadelphia Inquirer; Newsday; The Chronicle of Higher Education; Crain's;* The Associated

Press; Dow Jones; Reuters; Bloomberg Television; Bloomberg Radio; NPR; PBS; *Publishers Weekly; The Christian Science Monitor; The New York Post;* as well as Canadian, Latin American, and European newspapers, and so on.

His books, book chapters, and articles are or have been required or recommended reading at Harvard, Northwestern (Kellogg), UCLA (Anderson Graduate School of Business Administration), Columbia Graduate Business School, NYU, Brown, Rochester, Virginia, William & Mary, and more than 40 other colleges and universities in the U.S., Europe, and Asia.

He has done publishing industry consulting work for Goldman Sachs, JP Morgan; Morgan Stanley; Boston Consulting; Deutsche Bank; D.E. Shaw; Blackrock; The Blackstone Group; Bain Capital; Alliance Bernstein; Kohlberg, Kravis, & Roberts; Fidelity; MSD Capital; Booz Allen Hamilton; Bank of America; Citibank; McKinsey & Co.; Williams & Connolly LLP; Carter & English LLP; Accenture; *Foreign Affairs* (The Council on Foreign Relations); The National Endowment for the Arts; UNESCO; various NYC agencies; the Catholic University of America; The Library of Congress; and so on.

LIST OF TABLES

CHAPTER 1

Introduction: The State of the U.S. College Textbook Industry to 2000

Abstract The development of the oral tradition, the creation of scrolls, and eventually illuminated manuscripts were utilized in the ancient and medieval eras to educate students. After about 1450, written textbooks were utilized in various medieval universities (e.g., Oxford in 1167) to educate students in the humanities, the social sciences, and the sciences. These early textbooks were printed using the time-consuming letter-press process, effectively making these textbooks expensive for faculty members, libraries, or students. Once colleges were created in North America (e.g., Harvard in 1636), there was a pressing need for printed texts; for decades, printed books were imported from Europe even after the first book was printed in what is now the U.S. (e.g., the *Bay Psalm Book* in 1640). The creation of viable printing and publishing operations and the growth in both college enrollments and the number of colleges, in the years before, during, and after the end of World War II, triggered demand for college texts and related ancillary products, compelling college textbook publishers to adopt more effective production, distribution, marketing, and financial control procedures. By 2000, the financial state of the U.S. college textbook business was impressive, and the major textbook publishers were very optimistic about continued growth in the twenty-first century.

© The Author(s), under exclusive license to Springer Nature Switzerland AG 2023
A. N. Greco, *The College Textbook Publishing Industry in the U.S. 2000–2022*, Marketing and Communication in Higher Education, https://doi.org/10.1007/978-3-031-30415-6_1

Keywords Texts • Textbooks • College textbooks • Marketing strategies

HISTORICAL DEVELOPMENT OF EDUCATIONAL MATERIALS AND HIGHER EDUCATION TEXTBOOKS

"Texts" utilized in the ancient eras were oral versions of religious, educational, literary, or scientific materials.[1] Written scrolls, "a roll constructed of material that ranged from papyrus to parchment," were also utilized in the ancient world.[2]

During the medieval period in Europe, a number of important universities were established, including Bologna (in 1088), Paris (1150), and Oxford (1167).[3] Most students at these universities relied on the oral presentations of materials by "masters," and, if they were fortunate, a student might have access to illuminated manuscripts.[4]

The creation of these great medieval universities marked a substantive turning point in the development of higher education and, ultimately, the history of "textbooks."[5] For example, during the middle ages, students at Oxford University studied philosophy, the sciences, and the arts. Oral examinations of students were conducted by masters knowledgeable in their field.[6]

However, the development of the printed book in Germany (about 1450) transformed education and reading in Western Europe and, ultimately, in the entire world. While Gutenberg has been viewed as the inventor of the letterpress printing press (his press was based on the mechanics of the wine press) using movable type,[7] Elizbeth L. Eisenstein in *The Printing Press as an Agent of Change* insisted that other master printers also played a substantive role in the development of printing.[8]

European commercial printing operations emerged after Gutenberg's successful printing of the *Bible*.[9] William Caxton brought the printing press to England, printing the works of Chaucer, Cicero, Vergil, and so on, and these texts were used in some of that nation's colleges.[10] Lisa Jardine, in *Worldly Goods: A New History of the Renaissance*, wrote that technological developments allowed printers to print 300 to 400 copies of a title; however, the purchase of books remained a substantial investment. "In Venice around 1500 these [book] purchases represented about a week's salary for a teacher or skilled artisan."[11]

Since printed books were needed for university education, a small number of universities launched "university presses." Oxford created its university press in 1478.[12] Once it was operational, Oxford needed a retail establishment to sell its books to scholars, students, libraries, and the general public. So, while independent bookstores catered to the Oxford faculty and students, the university eventually opened its own bookshop.[13]

THE DEVELOPMENT OF COLLEGE TEXTBOOKS IN THE U.S.

Eventually, colleges were created in the American colonies, including Harvard College (in 1636) and the College of William and Mary (1693). The small number of colonial college instructors and students also needed educational materials, and for many years, textbooks printed and published originally in England were exported to the American colonies.

The first book printed in British North America (i.e., Colonial Massachusetts) was the religious *Bay Psalm Book*. "Printing the *Bay Psalm Book* in 1640 required importing the tools and materials of printing to the new colony... It was, nevertheless, the first full venture of printing in British North America, and this ambitious effort is an important monument of the establishment of this nation and its culture. It is estimated that 1700 copies of the book were printed, which sold for twenty pence. Today, only eleven copies survive."[14]

As in England, the early colonial colleges relied on college or independent bookstores to supply faculty and students with textbooks. Moravian College (established in 1742) opened its own college bookstore, which is the oldest, continuously operating college bookstore in the U.S.[15] While many textbooks were imported from England or, in some instances, from Europe, eventually American printing companies started printing textbooks, including John Wiley & Sons (established in 1807 during the presidential administration of Thomas Jefferson).[16]

College enrollments were rather small in the U.S. for most of the nineteenth century. According to the U.S. Department of Education's (Education) National Center for Education Statistics (NCES), in the 1869–1870 academic year, there were only 563 colleges in the U.S., instructing a total of 62,869 students (i.e., full-time undergraduate, graduate, and professional school students) and employing an instructional (i.e., faculty members) staff of 5553. The number of colleges grew slowly in the following decades, reaching 977 institutions in 1899–1900; 1041 colleges in 1919–1920; and 1708 colleges in 1939–1940.[17] The need for college textbooks grew in the years after 1636, albeit very slowly.

U.S. College Growth After 1941

World War II was a major turning point in the history of higher education in the U.S. Many colleges sustained serious declines in the number of students, staff, administrators, and faculty members when many of them entered the U.S. military (over 16 million served in the military during the war). The U.S. Government allocated financial and human resources in order to utilize many college campuses and buildings for various military purposes (including research for the Manhattan Project that produced the atomic bomb in 1945). On June 22, 1944, President Franklin D. Roosevelt signed the "G.I. Bill" that provided financial support for returning veterans that wanted a college or a professional degree as well as technical training in various trades (e.g., automotive technology).[18]

Textbook Publisher Marketing Strategies After World War II

Because of the tremendous impact of the "G.I. Bill," the number of colleges and student enrollments surged in the years after 1946, and this triggered increased demand for college faculty members, facilities, academic programs, libraries, and textbooks.[19] To meet the demand for textbooks, college textbook publishing firms crafted intriguing and exceptionally successful portfolio strategies designed to publish textbooks in a variety of existing and new academic categories. This portfolio concept of developing a wide range of books was based on the premise that, in any year, adoptions could be up in one academic field (perhaps philosophy) and down in another field (perhaps British literature). This methodology provided some insurance, in essence a hedge, against the vagaries of the marketplace. It was based on rather successful portfolio strategies developed, for example, in the motion picture industry in the 1920s and 1930s (e.g., releasing films in different genres, including mysteries, comedies, crime, westerns, etc.) as well as financial research developed in the 1950s (e.g., the creation of financial conglomerates; International Telephone and Telegraph managed telephone systems in Cuba, operated a major hotel chain, and manufactured Twinkies and Wonder Bread).[20]

This meant that textbook publishers were rather adaptative releasing new and frequently revised textbooks (often every 3–5 years) in the humanities, the social sciences, and the sciences. To make sure a publishing company remained an adaptative operation, they utilized a network of sales representatives (called "reps" in the business) that attended scholarly conferences, sent out press releases and materials about new or updated versions of textbooks, and visited colleges to talk with faculty members about the company's textbooks. The goals of the representatives were to convince a faculty member (or in some instances a faculty department) to adopt a specific textbook published by the rep's company, and they also surveyed constantly the changing academic landscape to ascertain what new, innovative academic fields emerged and needed textbooks. So, many firms released textbook titles, in the years and decades after the end of World War II, in newly popular academic and highly specialized occupational fields (e.g., the building and technical trades, construction management).

In addition, publishers started to pay attention to the early innovative marketing theories of business school professors including Alfred D. Chandler (concerning crafting a strategy and then the structural elements needed to achieve the strategy), Ted Levitt (regarding "marketing myopia," the importance of being market and not product focused), and other academics with managerial and marketing theories.[21]

The goal of adopting these business strategies was to achieve a competitive advantage, a unique value proposition, in the marketplace. In essence this meant delivering more value and satisfaction to faculty members and students while creating: an overall cost leadership position (i.e., to achieve scale; the lowest unit manufacturing and distribution costs for a text to increase profit margins), and gain market share. They needed a differentiated product line of textbooks to become the industry leader, and they crafted a "focus" on certain growing academic fields (e.g., business administration, law schools, and engineering). The architect of competitive strategy was Harvard Business School's Michael E. Porter. Porter insisted that a firm must have a clear strategy to achieve a superior performance and operational excellence. This meant attracting more users of a text (i.e., faculty adoptions) which generated ultimately more revenues and profits.[22]

In the late 1990s, the market for used or rental texts was rather small since college bookstores rarely had access to or provided an adequate supply of used or rental copies to satisfy student demands. Students often had to rely on visiting a rather small number of off-campus stores (e.g., The Strand Bookstore in New York City) that had used books, but these establishments primarily bought and sold used hardcover or paperback trade books. Very few had used textbooks for sale.

The Impact of Disruptive Technologies on Publishers and Textbook Sales

The launch of various online companies offering new and used hardcover and paperback trade books, and, at some point, used and rental textbooks were added, providing students with attractive albeit limited options to obtain a required text and save money. These new entitles included Amazon.com (it opened for business in a garage on July 5, 1994), eBay (September 3, 1995), and the innovative search engine Google (it also started in a garage on September 4, 1998). As textbooks were added by these and other online sites, students had access to easy to use online platforms to search for and purchase used and rental textbooks, an example of "frictionless commerce."

While textbook publishers were aware of these "disruptive" technologies in the late 1990s,[23] they did not believe these sites posed an immediate threat to their basic business model because of "traditional" processes and procedures. After all, a college faculty member adopted a specific textbook(s); he or she then submitted a textbook request form to the college bookstore which ordered the text(s); and students either decided to purchase the text(s) at the convenient on-campus bookstore or an off-campus independent bookstore (e.g., some colleges, for example, the City University of New York's John Jay College, relied for a number of years on off-campus bookstores rather than providing an on-campus one), use a library copy, or possibly share a title with another student. In any case, it was often rather difficult for the majority of students to pass a course without access to the required textbook, and the college bookstore either had on hand, or could easily acquire from the publisher or one of the many regional or national textbook distributors, a new copy of the required textbook.

While competition between the various publishers was rather keen, the end result clearly was the fact that textbook publishers were "cash cows" releasing new and revised versions of textbooks while generating annually impressive revenues and profits.

The U.S. Higher Education Textbook Industry in 2000

According to all of the available statistical data, the U.S. college textbook industry was in very good shape in 2000. The U.S. Department of Education (Education), National Center for Education Statistics (NCES), reported that in 2000 there were 15,312,289 students (i.e., customers for their textbooks) enrolled in U.S. colleges, and the vast majority were full-time students (58.84%) versus a number of part-time students (41.16%); annual enrollment increases were anticipated; and steady financial growth was projected by both higher education experts in the college bookstore sector and the major publishing associations. However, digital textbooks (i.e., e-textbooks) were "rare" in 2000. In 2000, U.S. textbook publishers released 5559 new and revised printed hardcover and paperback texts, and total new net text revenues topped $3.24 billion.[24]

To make sure that sales and profits continued unabated, textbook publishers utilized the classic "castle and moat" strategy. The "castle" was a textbook (e.g., *Principles of Marketing*) often written by a brand-name marketing author (e.g., Philip Kotler). The publisher's "moat" (i.e. the protective ring surrounding a textbook) comprised the company's intensive sales efforts (i.e., booths at major academic conferences and frequent visits to faculty offices) and the book's copyright (i.e., the legal "moat" protecting the textbook from copyright infringement). However, the basic sales and marketing procedures utilized by publishers were challenging because their editors had to estimate, perhaps three to five years in advance, what textbook faculty members would adopt, creating what economists call "dual sided uncertainty."[25]

SAMPLE PROFIT AND LOSS ANALYSIS FOR A COLLEGE TEXTBOOK IN 2000

In order to understand the higher education textbook sector, it is important to perceive how textbook publishers viewed the economics of publishing. The following material was based on public information as well as interviews, over a period of more than 27 years, with college book store retailers and textbook sales representatives.

Once an editor found a potential author(s), a book proposal and a potential profit and loss statement (P & Ls) were evaluated to determine the economic viability of the proposed book. If the financial projections were acceptable, a textbook contract and (usually) an advance (against future royalties) would be paid to the author (generally in two installments: when the contract was signed and when the manuscript was accepted for publication by the publisher).

A representative sample P & L is in Table 1.1, and this is a "typical" printed hardcover chemistry textbook published in 2000. Chemistry was selected since it is an important academic field for students in biology, physics, engineering, pre-med, nursing, pharmacy, and in the other health fields. Some liberal arts students take chemistry to fulfill a required science course. In 2000, thirty-five new or revised chemistry books (introductory and advanced) titles were published. Since books were released generally in a three cycle, in 1999 publishers released 64 new chemistry texts, and 47 were published in 2001. The three-year total (1999–2001) was 146 new chemistry books.[26]

This P & L was for a text in a three-year revision cycle, so, the initial print run was for 100,000 printed copies based on potential faculty adoptions. A standard percentage of the print run was allocated for "free" copies for sales representatives, faculty members, office use, and so on. So, the potential gross sales were 98,500 copies (also called units in the book publishing industry; units and copies were used interchangeably in this book). Actual U.S. sales totaled 89,000 units, and 16,020 copies were returned to the warehouse, netting 72,980 copies. Assuming the college bookstore (i.e., the retailer) complied with a publisher's terms and conditions of sale, a book is fully returnable for a complete refund; damaged books (called "dinks" in the business) were always returnable. So, in essence books were sold on consignment to a retailer. The suggested retail price (SRP) in the U.S. was $110.00, the average price for chemistry texts in 2000. However, a retailer can charge legally any price for a book, and many do.

In 2000, texts were sold into the channels of distribution, primarily college bookstores, at a discount. The "average" textbook discount for college or independent bookstores, according to the National Association of College Stores (NACS; the nation's leading college bookstore trade association), averaged about 23% of the suggested retail price. So, this $110.00 chemistry text netted the publisher $84.70 per unit.[27] Export sales reached 25,170 units, and 350 copies never shipped and remained in the warehouse. This text had a 50% export discount rate ($55.00 net to the publisher), but these copies were final sales (i.e., non-returnable except for "dinks").

Unit manufacturing costs (UMC based on industry averages in 2000) were printing, paper, and binding (known as PPB in the industry), $26.40; plant (i.e., editorial, art, design, page lay-out, and page make-up), $5.80; and marketing (sales representatives, direct mail, catalogues, academic conference booths, marketing personnel, etc.), $10.64. During the years before and after 2000, some textbook publishing companies shifted printing out of the U.S. to various Asian (e.g., Chinese) printing companies. The goal was to reduce unit manufacturing expenditures, creating a "defensive" position in the marketplace, and, hopefully, sparking an increase in market share and profit margins. However, while PPB costs were lower in Asia, there were some concerns. First, there was an inevitable lag in receiving these books in the U.S. since books were transported on ships. Second, the textbooks had to go through U.S. Customs, and this generated additional costs to the publishing firm. It had to purchase a "surety bond" to ensure that any tariff(s) on imported textbooks were paid by the publisher. C.A. Shea & Company, Inc., one of the leading surety bond companies in the U.S., outlined the purpose of a surety bond, sometimes called a "Customs Bond." "Anyone wishing to import goods into the United States or engage in import related operations is required to post some form of financial security with U.S. Customs and Border Protection (CBP). While CBP is authorized to accept a variety of forms of security... the most common (and typically most cost effective) form is a surety bond (Customs Bond). This posting protects the Customs revenue and ensures compliance with the regulations of the United States pertaining to importing and related activities."[28]

A college bookstore under management to an outside company (e.g., Barnes & Noble, also known as B & N; or Follett) paid "franchise fees" to the college to run their bookstore. These fees were never made public, but interviews with college bookstore managers indicated that they were frequently a percentage of gross sales. College textbook returns from B & N or Follett in 2000 were "high," sometimes topping 20%; however, certain academic disciplines posted lower rates (e.g., science; accounting).

U.S. net sales (i.e., gross sales minus returns equals net sales) of the chemistry text in Table 1.1 reached 72,980 copies, generating $6,181,406, and export tallies reached $1,384,359. Total net sales were $7,565,756. The cost of goods sold (i.e., COGS) totaled $3,950,038: PPB $2,640,000, plant $580,000, the author's earned royalty $715,044, and inventory write-off of unsold copies reached $14,994. Publisher interviews revealed that companies tried to avoid inventory write-offs since this accounting charge impacted negatively the book's bottom line. Corporate charges were $2,577,151, including marketing expenditures of $1,064,000 and corporate overhead of $1,513,151 (i.e., the firm's expenses for rent or mortgages, utilities, insurance, information technology, legal, executive

Table 1.1   Sample P & L for a printed hardcover chemistry textbook (with a three-year sales cycle) in 2000

Assumptions	
736 page black & white and color text; four-color photographs, illustrations, and statistical tables; table of contents, glossary, and index; fine heavy paper; each copy weighs 3.6 pounds	
Print run	100,000 copies
Free copies	1500 [author, editor, publishing house, sales representatives, faculty members for adoption review]
Gross sales	98,500 copies
Shipped	
U.S.	89,000 shipped copies
	16,020 returned copies [U.S. 18.00% return rate; industry average for science textbooks in 2000]
	72,980 net
Exports	25,170
	0 returned copies [exports; sold as final sales]
	25,170 net
Never shipped	350 copies
Suggested retail price (SRP)	$110.00
Average discount	23 percent [U.S. $84.70 @ net to publisher]
	50 percent [exports $55.00 @ net to publisher]
PPB	$26.40 [24 percent of SRP; per unit × 100,000 copies]
Plant	$5.80 [5.27 percent of SRP; per unit × 100,000 copies]
Marketing	$10.64 [9.67 percent of SRP; per unit × 100,000 copies]
Royalty advance	$500,0000.00 [an advance against royalty rate of 10 percent domestic and 7 percent of exports; net price]
Other publishing income	$0
Total Net Revenues	
1. Sales: U.S.	$6,181,406.00 [89,000–16,020 = 72,980 × $84.70]
2. Sales: exports	$1,384,350.00 [25,170 × $55.00]
3. Total sales	$7,565,756.00 [#1 + #2 = #3]
Cost of Goods Sold [COGS]	
4. PPB	$2,640,000.00 [$26.40 per unit × 100,000 copies]

(*continued*)

Table 1.1 (continued)

Assumptions	
5. Plant	$580,000.00 [$5.80 per unit × 100,000 copies]
6. Earned royalty	$715,044.00 [total] [$618,140.00; 10 percent U.S. sales + $96,904.00; 7 percent of export sales]
7. Royalty write-off	$0.00 [Difference between advance and earned royalty]
8. Inventory write-off	$14,994.00 [350 never shipped copies remained in warehouse; PPB $26.40+ $5.80 Plant +$10.64 marketing = $42.84 × 350]
9. Total COGS	$3,950,038.00 [#4 + #5 + #6 +#7 + #8 = #9]
Corporate Charges	
10. Marketing	$1,064,000.00 [$10.64 per unit × 100,000 copies]
11. Overhead 20% of total sales	$1,513,151.00 [20% of sales]
12. Total corporate charges	$2,577,151.00 [#10 + #11 = #12]
13. Total Sales	$7,565,756.00
14. Minus COGS	-$3,950,038.00
15. Minus corporate charges	-$2,577,151.00
16. Net profit	$1,038,567.00
17. Profit margin	13.73%

N.B. All numbers were rounded off and may not always equal 100 percent. The average SRP for a chemistry textbook in 2000 was $109.93; see Bogart, D. ed. *The Bowker Annual: Library and Book Trade Almanac 2002 47th Edition* (Medford, NJ: Information Today, Inc., 2002), page 534. All numbers were rounded off in this P & L. Average "return percentage rate" for a chemistry book in 2000 was used. "Overhead" includes general and administrative expenses, shipping, fulfillment costs, etc. "PPB" refers to printing, paper, and binding costs. "Plant" refers to editorial, art, design, and page make-up expenses. "Marketing" includes all marketing and sales expenses. Industry averages in 2000 were used to determine PPB, Plant, and Marketing costs. "Inventory write-off" (w/o) assumes no remainder income. All textbooks are returnable for full credit, assuming the bookstore or wholesaler complies with the publisher's terms and conditions of sale. The author received an advance (against royalties) of $500,000.00; $250,000.00 was paid when the contract was signed; the remaining $250,000.00 was paid when the manuscript was received and accepted by the publisher. Additional payments were made annually (totaling $215,040.00) since the royalty rate exceeded the guaranteed advance.

salaries and fringe benefits, fulfillment and distribution, taxes, interest costs, etc.).

This was a very successful textbook generating $1,038,571 in profits and a profit margin of 13.73%. Unfortunately, not every text is this successful since a rather small percentage of all textbooks generate large profits and margins (the famous "Pareto Power Law" concept). "Star" authors, with a "brand name" (e.g., an academic with prestigious publications or the winner of a major scholarly award) commanded advances and royalty rates significantly larger than those in this P & L. For example, in 1996, a college textbook publisher paid Harvard economist N. Gregory Mankiw (formerly Chair of the U.S. Council of Economic Advisors between May 29, 2003, and February 18, 2005), and a well-known "academic star," $1.4 million (about $2.66 million in 2023 dollars) to write what became a bestselling economics textbook.[29] One "estimate" indicated that Mankiw's royalties for this book, in its 9th (2020) edition with millions of copies sold [e.g., in 2022 a new copy of this text had a suggested retail price, SRP, of $175.99], might have exceeded $42 million.[30]

How can a publisher recoup this type of an advance? The typical marketing strategy was to release new and revised editions of a successful textbook perhaps every 3–5 years, craft innovative sales strategies, send direct mail information about a new edition to faculty members, place ads in scholarly journals, offer free textbooks or samples at academic conferences, utilize sales calls on faculty members, raise prices, and sell tens of thousands of copies. Once a text is adopted by an individual faculty member (or, at many colleges, by a faculty committee), the sales representative makes sure that free ancillary documents (e.g., the teacher's editions, computer-generated tests, PowerPoint slides, chapter outlines, etc.) were sent to or made available to instructors. The costs for the ancillaries were added to the text's SRP. This overarching strategy, with certain borderline chaotic characteristics impacted by faculty turnovers due to retirements or leaves, worked in the 1990s and the early 2000s. This was because many publishers often had sizable export sales, especially in biology, chemistry, physics, finance, economics, marketing information technology, and English language titles. Unfortunately, foreign markets required sizable expenses to reach faculty members outside the U.S.[31]

Conclusion

So, by the end of the 1999–2000 academic year, the U.S. textbook publishing industry was very profitable and well entrenched in academia. However, the basic textbook business model rested firmly on a "product" orientation (i.e., a college textbook, ancillary products) and not on a "market" student end-user oriented strategy, a concern analyzed by Levitt. These publishers have mastered editing, printing, publishing, distribution, and selling textbooks. They knew basically what faculty members wanted, yet they did not undertake surveys of what students really wanted and needed. In addition, many publishers did not pay attention to the growing chorus of textbook critics inside and outside academia voicing concerns and complaints about they viewed as the never-ending increases in textbook prices.

So, this very successful and lucrative college textbook business model would be tested and in many instances undermined, by intriguing online websites, using dynamic pricing strategies (i.e., an online price could change within a matter of seconds, known as "frictionless commerce"), and these sites slowly but efficiently acquired exceptionally important data about student purchases as well as used textbooks that could be sold or rented to students often at very low prices.

Economists have long debated whether consumers were rational.[32] It appears that, in the years after 2000, students were rational; they looked for a required textbook (new, used, or rented) at the best possible price regardless of retail venue. And a plethora of online retail establishments emerged devoted to satisfying the textbook wants and needs of students. So, the well-established world of college textbook publishing in 2000 would be challenged in the coming years by disruptive technologies and companies looking for market share, revenues, and profits in the textbook sector.

NOTES

1. R. Thomas. *Literacy and Orality in Ancient Greece* (Cambridge: Cambridge University Press, 2010), pp. 15–28, 52–73, 158–170.
2. *Ibid.*
3. H. Rashdall. *The Universities of Europe in the Middle Ages* (Oxford: Oxford University Press, 1995), pp. 17–53. Also see A.B. Cobban. *English University Life in the Middle Ages* (Columbus: Ohio State University Press, 1999), pp. 45–168. S. Ferruolo. *The Origins of the University: The Schools of Paris and their Critics, 1100–1215* (Stanford: Stanford University Press, 1998), pp. 87–126.
4. C. de Hamel. "A History of Illuminated Manuscripts," *Leonardo, 20,* 1(1987), 100–103.
5. J.L. Catto and R. Evans (eds). *The History of the University of Oxford Vol 11: Late Medieval Oxford* (Oxford: Oxford University Press, 1993), pp. 42–125,288–321.
6. *Ibid.*

7. S. Fussel. *Gutenberg and the Impact of Printing* (Aldershot, UK: Ashgate Publishing, 2005), pp. 35–73, 141–159. Also see M.E. Suarez, H.R. Wooudhuysen. *The Book: A Global History* (Oxford: Oxford University Press, 2013), pp. 351–657.

8. E.L. Eisenstein. *The Printing Press as an Agent of Change* (Cambridge: Cambridge University Press, 1980), pp. xv, 3–42. Also see Elizabeth Eisenstein. *The Printing Revolution in Early Modern Europe* (Cambridge: Cambridge University Press, 2012), pages 20–115. J.E. Dittmar. "Information Technology and Economic Change: The Impact of the Printing Press," *Quarterly Journal of Economics 126* (2011): 1133–1172.

9. S. Echard. *Printing in the Middle Ages* (Philadelphia: University of Pennsylvania Press 2008), pp. vii-xvi, 60–96, 126–161. Also see B. Dietz. "Towards a History of Scientific Publishing," *History of Science*, 60, 2 (2022), pp. 155–165. N. Howard. *Loath to Print: The Reluctant Scientific Author 1500–1750* (Baltimore, MD: Johns Hopkins University Press, 2022), pp. 51–220.

10. A.S.G. Edwards. "William Caxton and the Introduction of Printing to England," The British Library, www.bl.uk/medieval-literature/articles/william-caxton-and-the-introduction-of-printing-to-england

11. L. Jardine. *Worldly Goods: A New History of the Renaissance* (New York: Doubleday, 1995), p. 160.

12. Oxford University Press. A Short History of Oxford University Press; https://global.oup.com/about/oup_history/?cc=us

13. *Ibid.*

14. The Library of Congress. "First Among Many: The Bay Psalm Book and Early Moments in American Printing," www.loc.gov/exhibits/bay-psalm-book-and-american-printing/online-exhibition.html. Also see J. Tebbel. *A History of Book Publishing in the United States: Volume I The Creation of an Industry 1630–1865* (New York: R.R. Bowker, 1972), pp. 90–91, 109–110, 112–115, 119. A.M.E. Morris. "The Art of Purifying: The Bay Psalm Book and Colonial Puritanism," *Early American Literature 42*, 1(2007): 107–130. H. Amory. "Printing and Bookselling in New England, 1638–1713," in H. Amory and D.D. Hall, eds. *A History of the Book in America, Vol. 1 The Colonial Book in the Atlantic World* (Cambridge, U.K.: Cambridge University Press, 2000), pages 83–116; P. Miller. *The New England Mind: The Seventeenth Century* (Cambridge: Harvard University Press, 1954), pages 73–90; H. Amory. "'Gods Altar Needs Not Our Pollishings:' Revisiting the Bay Psalm Book." *Printing History* 12 (1990): 2–14. Of the *Bay Psalm Book's* original print run of 1700 copies, printed in quarto on a letterpress press, only 11 copies are known still to exist, and only 5 are complete copies of the book. On November 26, 2013, "at Sotheby's New York, one of only 11 surviving copies of the Bay Psalm

Book set a then new world auction record for any printed book when it sold for $14,165,000. The book was purchased by American businessman and philanthropist David Rubenstein, who plans to share it with the American public by loaning it to libraries across the country, before putting it on long-term loan at one of them," http://www.sothebys.com/en/auctions/2013/the-bay-psalm-book-sale-n09039.html

15. S. Novak. "A Brief History of the Moravian Book Shop: Among the Oldest Bookstores in the World," www.lehighvalleylive.com/bethlehem/2018/05/a_brief_history_of_the-moravian.html

16. W.S. Reese. "The First Hundred Years of Printing in British North America: Printers and Collectors," American Antiquarian Society, www.americanantiquarian.org/proceedings/44539460.pdf. Also see John Wiley & Sons. *The First One Hundred and Fifty Years: A History of John Wiley and Sons, Incorporated, 1807–1957* (New York: John Wiley & Sons, 1957), pp. 1–24. G.B. Nash. *First City: Philadelphia and the Forging of Historical Memory* (Philadelphia: University of Pennsylvania Press, 2002), pages 38–113. F.L. Mott. *American Journalism: A History, 1690–1960* (New York: Macmillan, 1962), pages 404–405. C.A. Madison. *Book Publishing in America* (New York: McGraw-Hill, 1966), page 132.

17. U.S. Department of Education. National Center for Education Statistics (NCES). "120 Years of American Education: A Statistical Portrait;" nces.ed.gov/pubs93/93442.pdf. Table 303.10. Total fall enrollment in degree-granting postsecondary institutions, by attendance, sex of student, and control of institution. Selected years 1947 through 2026; www.nces.ed.gov/programs/digest/d18/tables/dt18_303.10.asp

18. U.S. Department of Defense (Defense). "75 Years of the GI Bill: How Transformative it's Been;" www.defense.gov/Explore/Features/story/Article/1727086/75-years-of-the-gi-bill-how-transformative-its-been

19. For U.S. textbook revenues between 1950 and 1960, see A. Bing. "Educational publishing: Problems and Prospects," *The American Behavioral Scientist*, 6, 3(1962), 20–23. Also see P. Whitten. "Textbook Publishing in the 1970s," *The Annals of the American Academy of Political and Social Science*, 421 (September 1975), 56–66. G.T. Sewall. "Textbook Publishing," *The Phi Delta Kappan*, 86, 7(March 2005), 498–502. J.M. Reed. "The History of the Textbook: The State of the Discipline," *Book History* 21 (2018), 397–424. Tebbel. *A History of Book Publishing in the United States: Volume II The Expansion of an Industry 1865–1919* (New York: R.R. Bowker,1975), pp. 10, 13–14, 16, 68, 100, 104, 113, 152, 293–294, 483, 565, 574. Tebbel. *A History of Book Publishing in the United States: Volume III The Golden Age Between Two World Wars 1920–1940* (New York: R.R. Bowker, 1978), pp. 53, 55, 396–397, 403–405, 467–468, 498. H.J. Addison. "Books and Bucks: The Economics

of College Textbook Publishing. *College Composition and Communication*, 23, 3 (1972): 287–291; https://www.jstor.org/stable/356663

20. H.L. Vogel. *Entertainment Industry Economics: A Guide for Financial Analysis, 4th edition* (New York: Cambridge University Press, 1998), pp., 52–56. Also see S. Sparviero. "The Business Strategy of Hollywood's Most Powerful Distributors: An Empirical Analysis," *Observatorio*, 7, 4(2013), 45–62. For financial portfolio analysis, see H.M. Markowitz. "Portfolio Selection," *Journal of Finance*, 7, 1(March 1952), 77–91. F.J. Fabozzi, F. Gupta, H.M. Markowitz. "The Legacy of Modern Portfolio Theory," *The Journal of Investing*, 11, 3, (Fall 2002), 7–22. E. Fama. "Portfolio Analysis in a Stable Parentian Market," *Management Science* 11, 3 (January 1965), 404–421.

21. The best sources of business strategies include A.D. Chandler. *Strategy and Structure: Chapters in the History of the American Industrial Enterprise* (Cambridge: MIT Press, 1962), pp. 1–17. T. Levitt. "Marketing Myopia," *Harvard Business Review*, 53, 5 (1975), 26. R.H. Hayes, W.J. Abernathy. "Managing Our Way to Economic Decline," *Harvard Business Review*, 58, 4 (1980), 68. E.J. McCarthy. *Basic Marketing, A Managerial Approach* (Burr Ridge, IL: Richard D. Irwin, 1960), pp. 14–62. M.G. Harvey, R.F. Lusch, B. Cavarkapa. "A Marketing Mix for the Twenty-First Century," *Journal of Marketing Theory and Practice*, 4, 4(Fall 1996), 4. M.E. Porter. "The Five Competitive Forces That Shape Strategy," *Harvard Business Review*, 86, 1(2008), 80. A.N. Greco. *The Business of Scholarly Publishing: Managing in Turbulent Times* (New York: Oxford University Press, 2020), pp. 1–12. Greco. "Economics of Publishing" in A. Phillips, M. Bhaskar, (eds.), *The Oxford Handbook of Publishing* (Oxford: U.K.: Oxford University Press, 2019), pp. 165–188. Greco. "The Strategy of Publishing" in Phillips, Bhaskar (eds.), *The Oxford Handbook of Publishing* (Oxford: U.K.: Oxford University Press, 2019), pp. 189–206.

22. Porter. *Competitive Strategy: Techniques for Analyzing Industries and Competitors* (New York: The Free Press, 1998), pp. 12–49. Also see Porter. *The Competitive Advantage: Creating and Sustaining Superior Performance* (New York: Free Press, 1985), pp. 45–78.

23. C.M. Christensen. *The Innovator's Dilemma: The Revolutionary Book That Will Change the Way You Do Business* (New York: Harper Business, 2011), pp. 1–116. Also see Christensen. "The Innovator's Dilemma: When New Technologies Cause Great Firms to Fail," https://www.hbs.edu/faculty/pages/item.aspx?num=46

24. U.S. Department of Commerce. Bureau of the Census. *Statistical Abstract of the United States 2020*. Section 4: Education. Table 321 bachelor's degrees earned by field: 1980 to 2017; Table 324 master's and doctoral degrees earned by field: 1971 to 2017; www.statabs-proquest-com.

avoserv2.library.fordham.edu/ftv2/4c4e000002b244ea20.pdf. Also see D. Bogart (ed.). *The Bowker Annual: Library and Book Trade Almanac 2002 47th Edition* (Medford, NJ: Information Today, Inc., 2002), pages 534–535, 554.

25. P.C. Cramton/"Strategic Delay in Bargaining with Two-Sided Uncertainty," *The Review of Economic Studies,* 59, 1(January 1992), 205–225.

26. Bogart (ed.). *The Bowker Annual: Library and Book Trade Almanac 2002 47th Edition* (Medford, NJ: Information Today, Inc., 2002), pages 534–535, 554.

27. National Association of College Stores, www.nacs.org/research/HigherEdRetailMarketFactsFigures.aspx

28. For information about surety bonds, see C.A. Shea & Company, Inc.. "Custom Bonds," www.cashea.com/customs-bonds

29. A. Schneider. "A Harvard Economist Hits the Jackpot with a $1.4 Million Advance for a Textbook," *The Chronicle of Higher Education,* www.chronicle.com/article/A-Harvard-Economist-Hits-the/98276

30. R. Reed. "A $280 College Textbook Busts Budgets, but Harvard Author Gregory Mankiw Defends Royalties," www.oregonlive.com/education/2015/02/a_$280_college_textbook_busts_b.html. Also see T. Wu. "How College Professors Rip Off Students," www.nytimes.com/2019/12/11/opinion/textbooks-prices-college.html

31. Bogart. *The Bowker Annual: Library and Book Trade Almanac 2002 47th Edition,* pages 534–535, 554.

32. P.J. Hammond. "Rationality in Economics," web.stanford.edu/~hammond/ratEcon.pdf. Also see D. Ariely. "The End of Rational Economics," hbr.org/2009/07/the-end-of-rational-economics

CHAPTER 2

The Impact of Disruption on the College Textbook Publishing Industry: 2001–2012

Abstract Higher education in the U.S. experienced a period of impressive growth after 2000. However, a series of unanticipated challenges undermined and threatened the basic business models that worked so successfully between 1945 and 2000. The challenges that emerged between 2001 and 2012 included an insidious recession, sagging sales of new printed textbooks, student enrollment declines in 2011 and 2012, and the emergence of easy to use online operations offering students deep discounts for used and rental college textbooks impacted both publisher's revenues and unit sales. The major textbook publishers attempted to address these concerns with a series of interesting but ultimately unsuccessful marketing and production strategies.

Keywords College enrollments • Textbook revenues • Suggested retail prices • Textbook publishers • Disruptive technologies

A Period of Confidence After 2000

The future isn't what it used to be.
Yogi Berra (U.S. Baseball Hall of Fame Player)[1]

The U.S. college textbook industry was exceptionally optimistic about their business opportunities in the twenty-first century. After all, their

19

A. N. Greco, *The College Textbook Publishing Industry in the U.S. 2000–2022*, Marketing and Communication in Higher Education, https://doi.org/10.1007/978-3-031-30415-6_2

basis business strategy worked, and almost all of the available statistical data supported their belief in the efficiency of their business models. Total college enrollments posted impressive annual increases: between 2000 and 2005, +14.21% (the brief recession between March and November 2001 dampened sales slightly) and during the years 2005–2009, +20.20%. However, the high point in total enrollments was 2010 (21,019,438). Declines were posted for the after 2010: –0.04% in 2011, and more slippage in 2012 (–1.74%). Table 2.1 has the details.

During those same years, new textbook revenues increased between 2000 and 2005, +4.94%, and in 2005–2009, +26.47%. The recession between December 2007 and June 2009 did not impact negatively textbook revenue totals because there was an increase in total student enrollment (which often occurs when unemployed or underemployed individuals decide to return to college, professional, or graduate school to get another degree).[2] However, a closer analysis of new textbook unit sales revealed

Table 2.1 Total U.S. non-profit public and private college students: 2000–2012

Year	Undergraduate and graduate students			Total annual percentage change
	Full-time	Part-time	Total	
2000	9,009,600	6,302,689	15,312,289	–
2001	9,447,502	6,480,485	15,927,987	+4.02%
2002	9,946,359	6,665,352	16,611,711	+4.29%
2003	10,326,133	6,585,348	16,911,481	+1.80%
2004	10,610,177	6,661,867	17,272,044	+2.13%
2005	10,797,011	6,690,464	17,487,475	+1.25%
2006	10,957,536	6,796,692	17,754,230	+1.53%
2007	11,270929	6,987,209	18,258,138	+2.84%
2008	11,734636	7,347,050	19,081,686	+4.51%
2009	12,605,355	7,708,239	20,313,594	+6.46%
2010	13,087,182	7,932,256	21,019,438	+3.47%
2011	13,002,531	8,008,059	21,010,590	–0.04%
2012	12,734,404	7,910,074	20,644,478	–1.74%
Percent change 2000–2012	+41.34%	+25.50%	+34.82%	–

U.S. Department of Education. National Center for Education Statistics, https://nces.ed.gov/programs/digest/d18/tables/dt18_303.10.asp

N.B. All numbers were rounded off and may not always equal 100%

the beginning of "structural weakness" in many of the textbook publisher's basic business model. Textbook revenues between 2000 and 2012 posted a +32.41% increase, lagging slightly behind the total increase in the Consumer Price Index (CPI) at +33.33%. However, 2010 was also the peak year in terms of revenues $4.49 billion, up from $3.24 billion in 2000 (+38.58%). Declines were reported for both 2011 ($4.52 billion; −3.62% from 2010) and 2012 ($4.29 billion; −5.09% from 2011). Table 2.2 has textbook revenues.

Unit sales of hardcover textbooks increased a modest +4.90% between 2000 and 2005, and paperback totals were slightly better with a +5.04% increase. Total hardcover and paperback textbook tallies for the years 2005–2009 were underwhelming, and both textbook formats posted an increase of only +2.67%. However, very modest tallies were recorded for

Table 2.2 U.S. net college new textbook revenues: 2000–2012 ($ billions), and the Consumer Price Index (CPI): 2000–2012

Year	New textbook revenues	Consumer Price Index (CPI)
2000	$3.24	172.2
2001	$3.47	177.1
2002	$3.90	179.9
2003	$3.39	184.0
2004	$3.45	188.9
2005	$3.40	195.3
2006	$3.50	201.6
2007	$3.70	207.3
2008	$3.81	215.3
2009	$4.30	214.5
2010	$4.69	218.1
2011	$4.52	224.9
2012	$4.29	229.6
Percent change 2000–2012	+32.41%	+33.33%

Source: The Association of American Publishers (AAP). Also see AAP datasets in Publishers Weekly, various issues. *The Bowker Annual* and *The Library and Book Trade Almanac*, various years. The Federal Reserve Bank of Minneapolis. The Consumer Price Index (CPI). Base year 1982–1984 = 100

www.minneapolisfed.org/about-us/monetary-policy/inflation-calculator/consumer-price-index-1913

N.B. All numbers were rounded off and may not always equal 100%. Gross sales minus returns equals net revenues

Table 2.3   U.S. new college textbook unit sales by print format: 2000–2012 (in millions)

Year	Hardcover net	Paperbacks net	Total
2000	28.6	35.7	64.3
2001	29.9	36.9	66.8
2002	30.6	37.8	68.4
2003	30.9	38.3	69.2
2004	30.2	37.8	68.0
2005	30.0	37.5	67.6
2006	30.1	37.5	67.6
2007	30.3	37.9	68.2
2008	30.6	38.2	68.8
2009	30.8	38.5	69.4
2010	31.1	38.8	69.9
2011	31.3	39.1	70.4
2012	31.5	39.4	71.0
Total	395.9	493.4	889.6
Percent change 2000–2012	+10.14	+10.36	+10.42
Average annual percent change 2000–2012	+0.78	+0.8	+0.8

Source: Book Industry Study Group, Inc. (BISG). *Book Industry Trends;* various years. BISG data also appeared in various issues of *The Statistical Abstract of the United States, The Wall Street Journal, The New York Times,* etc. N.B. All textbook units are net units (i.e., total unit sales minus returns equals net units)

2011 (+0.72%) and 2012 (+0.85% over 2011's statistics). Table 2.3 has new college textbook hardcover and paperback unit sales totals for the years 2000–2012.

New textbook suggested retail prices (SRPs) increased to compensate for the decline in unit sales. The average suggested retail price between 2000 and 2005 for texts in the humanities surged +8.38%, with a staggering increase of +16.19% between 2005 and 2009 and another +13.33% between 2009 and 2012. This same pattern was evident in the social sciences (2000–2005: +7.67%; 2005–2009, +19.06%, but a more modest +5.84% between 2009 and 2012). The science and technology sector also recorded impressive SRP changes: 2000–5005, +19.91%; 2005–2009, +6.86%. However, the increase between 2009 and 2012 was only +0.41%. Table 2.4 has the totals.

Reliable statistical data was available for the average suggested prices in 32 distinct academic fields for college textbooks. Three "typical"

Table 2.4 Average suggested retail prices (SRPs) and new title output for new hardcover and paperback U.S. college textbook revenues in the humanities, the social sciences, and science and technology: 2000–2012 (U.S. dollars)

Year	Humanities SRP (new units)	Social sciences SRP (new units)	Science and technology SRP (new units)
2000	$48.32 (1963)	$47.31 (2645)	$55.41 (982)
2001	$48.05 (1988)	$47.93 (2647)	$54.51 (999)
2002	$49.57 (2050)	$47.10 (2873)	$53.41 (1063)
2003	$51.49 (2008)	$50.34 (2824)	$54.24 (1032)
2004	$52.64 (2061)	$50.66 (2789)	$61.77 (1132)
2005	$52.37 (2040)	$50.94 (2748)	$66.44 (1150)
2006	$55.11 (1975)	$52.98 (2775)	$67.06 (1046)
2007	$56.09 (2140)	$54.46 (2860)	$66.15 (1110)
2008	$58.37 (2013)	$56.40 (2924)	$67.34 (1326)
2009	$60.85 (1924)	$60.65 (2896)	$71.00 (1345)
2010	$61.60 (2002)	$59.09 (3052)	$67.13 (1309)
2011	$66.89 (2044)	$65.08 (3364)	$67.65 (1303)
2012	$68.96 (2121)	$64.19 (3057)	$71.29 (1163)
Percent change 2000–2012	+42.72	+35.68	+28.66
Total new title output	26,329	37,454	14,960

Source: *The Bowker Annual* and *The Library and Book Trade Almanac*, various years. N.B. *The Bowker Annual* changed its name to *The Library and Book Trade Almanac* in 2008. The number in the parentheses is new title output. These are average prices for hardcover and paperback textbooks. The average price for a hardcover text is higher than the cost for a paperback title

academic fields offered by the vast majority of undergraduate U.S. colleges were selected for analysis in the broadly defined liberal arts, the social sciences, and the science-technology (STM) fields, specifically: English and American literature, North American history, and chemistry. English and American literature increased +18.25% between 2000 and 2005, with an additional +16.36% change between 2005 and 2009. A more modest increase of +12.80% was evident between 2009 and 2012. While North American history's 2000–2005 change in the SRP grew only +7.03%, this sector posted a large increase between 2005 and 2009 of +20.86%. SRPs sagged to only +1.24% between 2009 and 2012. Chemistry textbook prices were impacted by the small number of new books released annually. Prices increased +10.32% between 2000 and 2005, but they dropped −15.20% during the years 2005–2009 and another draconian decline of −12.18% between 2009 and 2012. Table 2.5 has the details.

Table 2.5 Average suggested retail prices (SRPs) and new title output for new hardcover and paperback U.S. college textbook revenues in English and American literature, North American history, and chemistry: 2000–2012 (U.S. dollars)

Year	English and American literature SRP (new units)	North American history SRP (new units)	Chemistry SRP (new units)
2000	$45.60 (515)	$38.11 (431)	$109.93 (35)
2001	$30.27 (547)	$40.33 (364)	$82.99 (47)
2002	$49.62 (498)	$40.61 (348)	$90.75 (40)
2003	$53.42 (457)	$42.93 (388)	$101.29 (47)
2004	$52.14 (419)	$42.32 (413)	$114.08 (65)
2005	$53.92 (418)	$40.79 (380)	$121.84 (73)
2006	$57.36 (424)	$40.51 (396)	$110.55 (60)
2007	$57.70 (401)	$42.53 (406)	$116.67 (76)
2008	$58.83 (420)	$45.07 (382)	$109.05 (70)
2009	$62.74 (382)	$49.30 (396)	$103.32 (50)
2010	$61.96 (394)	$45.50 (444)	$115.42 (42)
2011	$68.92 (376)	$47.43 (445)	$90.06 (48)
2012	$70.77 (412)	$49.91 (416)	$90.74 (46)
Percent change 2000–2012	+55.20	+30.96	−17.46
Total new title output	5663	5209	699

Source: *The Bowker Annual* and *The Library and Book Trade Almanac*, various years. N.B. *The Bowker Annual* changed its name to *The Library and Book Trade Almanac* in 2008. The number in the parentheses is new title output. The average prices for hardcover and paperback textbooks. The average price for a hardcover text is higher than the cost for a paperback title

A review of public financial data for the five largest textbook publishers and annual textbook revenue tallies between 2000 and 2009 revealed relatively "consistent" market shares (N.B.: all numbers were rounded off, and a firm's market share could change annually). Pearson was the market leader holding a commanding 33% share of the entire college textbook market during the years 2000–2009; Cengage generally averaged a 21% share. McGraw-Hill hovered at the 15% mark, and Macmillan's share was a small but overall healthy 5%. John Wiley rounded out the top 5 with about 4%. With little or no annual changes in market share, the five largest textbook publishers (known as the "Big 5") generally accounted annually for about 80% of all higher education revenues. Other important college book publishers accounted for most of the remaining 20% of the market, including W.W. Norton, Oxford University Press, Routledge/Taylor & Francis, Edward Elgar, and a number of small, niche domestic and foreign publishers.

However, a series of apparently "unrelated" demographic, sales, and technological events took place that upended what had been a highly successful business for the five largest textbook publishers, and all of these publishers were hard pressed to understand and cope successfully with these developments.

THE IMPACT OF DISRUPTION

The highpoint of U.S. college enrollments was the year 2010, when totals peaked at 21,019,438 (+37.27% since 2000). In the following 2 years, education reported steady declines (−1.78%). New textbook revenues as well as new unit sales dropped to −8.53% between 2010 and 2012. However, substantive technological trends included the growing availability of light-weight portable laptops and tablets, and the emergence of new, innovative, and reliable online information search capabilities. These developments impacted ultimately students and the entire college textbook industry.

In the 1960s, the U.S. Department of Defense (Defense) began work on the ARPANET which formed the basis of the original and highly popular dial-up internet service launched by America On-Line (AOL, which was originally called ironically PlayNET), Yahoo, and Quantum Computer Services in the 1980s. By 2000, AOL was the largest internet company in the U.S. worth about $125 billion. Dial-up internet connections were slow and erratic, and many consumers used desk-top and laptop computers (e.g., the Commodore 64, the Osborne-1, and the famous and popular Radio Shack TRS-80) that had limited storage capacity, were very slow, used floppy disks, and were expensive. The launch of faster laptops, including the IBM PC (in 1986) and the Compaq SLT (1988) impacted positively consumers in both business and academia. The real game-changer was Apple with its stylish Macintosh (launched in a famous Super Bowl commercial in 1986) and the Powerbook (launched in 1991). Unfortunately, searching the internet was at times a difficult and exceptionally frustrating experience since consumers relied on the then available and often "inexact" search engines including AltaVista, Ask Jeeves, WebCrawler, MetaCrawler, and so on.[3]

In July 1995, three people working in a garage in Bellevue, WA, launched a company eventually called Amazon.com (its original name was Cadabra, a name that was rather confusing since some individuals thought the company was called "cadaver"), an event that almost surely escaped the attention of most textbook publishers and editors. Jeff Bezos, his then wife, and an employee sold books on this website. Eventually Amazon. com expanded its operations to include the sale of new and used trade, professional, and college textbooks, which Bezos viewed as commodities. He later added a large number of other products to this website (e.g., consumer packaged goods and appliances). While it took some time before Amazon became financially viable, the ability of college students to purchase new, rental, and used textbooks from Amazon and other online book sites (e.g., Chegg.com, Bookrenter.com, eBay, etc.) became rather appealing.[4]

However, search remained a serious problem until September 1998 when two graduate students working in a garage created a highly reliable, fast, and easy to use search engine that cut through the horrendous maze of useful and useless information appearing on the internet. These two people were Larry Page and Sergey Brin, and their company was Google. com. This new company experienced a period of unprecedented growth because Google was free, fast, and searched the internet efficiently to list a herculean amount of data and information. In addition, the company added attractive and free features including email, a calendar, storage, messaging, and so on.[5] Another significant development was the launch of faster laptops with more memory (e.g., IBM, Dell, H-P, and Apple).

There was great deal of interest in developing a smaller, efficient personal tablet, in essence a "computer," for consumers. Apple released its Apple Newton, which did not achieve a high level of popular support. Some technology companies released small portable, light-weight "netbooks" including the "Microsoft Tablet PC." The pivotal event was the launch in 2010 of the Apple iPad Tablet. While the original Apple iPad was rather heavy with a limited memory, it was immensely popular. Eventually, Apple increased the iPad's memory, speed, and features while reducing its weight, and Americans responded enthusiastically to tablets and iPads, including some that were not Apple products. Between 2010 and 2012, Americans purchased 74.3 million tablets, and 58 million were Apple iPad tablets.[6]

Because of major financial investments by large corporations (e.g., Verizon; AT & T) and significant technological improvements, dial-up internet access was replaced by fast wireless broadband.[7] While Palm Pilots and Blackberries were immensely popular, with an unbelievably devoted base of consumers, the introduction of the Apple smartphones impacted the entire portable phone sector with its attractive and sleek design, storage capacity, and search features. Eventually Apple added other well-received features (e.g., a camera, "find my phone," a compass, maps, a flashlight, etc.). By 2012 more than 680 million Apple smartphones were sold in the world.[8] Consumers also purchased other smartphones from competitive companies (e.g., Samsung).

Economic instability in the U.S. impacted events between 2001 and 2012. The nation's unemployment rate stood at 4.0% in 2000. However, recessions triggered increased unemployment tallies reaching 6.0% in 2003, declining to 4.6% in 2007, spiking to 9.6% in 2010, and inching downward to 8.1% in 2012.[9]

THE IMPACT OF DISRUPTION

While most textbook publishing firms were aware of the tremendous new technologies accepted by consumers, far too many publishers and editors failed to comprehend the short-term and long-term impact of what were clearly "disruptive technologies" on their business model. By 2012, the availability of laptops, tablets, and iPads with search capabilities changed the technological landscape at many American colleges and universities (especially in certain professional schools including medical, dental, nursing, engineering, business, and law schools). Now students could search quickly and efficiently with a few clicks on a keyboard going from one website to another looking for information about the best price for new, used, or rented college textbooks from a variety of online websites.[10]

Clayton M. Christensen wrote about "disruptive technologies" in his book *The Innovator's Dilemma: The Revolutionary Book That Will Change the Way You Do Business.* Christensen maintained that his research revealed that "it shows that in the case of well-managed firms... good management was the most powerful reason they failed ..."[11] He also wrote about "sustaining versus disruptive technologies" and "lessons for spotting disruptive threats."[12] Many of Christensen's theories were well received in U.S. and foreign business schools, sparking an outpouring of detailed industry studies.[13] However, there were vocal critics of Christensen's analyses of why good companies failed, including a major article by Jill Lepore in *The New Yorker.* Lepore insisted that "the handpicked case study, which is Christensen's method, is a notoriously weak foundation on which to build a theory."[14]

THE RESPONSE OF THE TEXTBOOK PUBLISHERS

The five largest college textbook publishers responded eventually to disruption in the marketplace with a series of interesting changes to their basic, well-entrenched business model. First, they decided to capitalize on some of these new technologies by releasing printed textbooks with CD-ROMs (generally in a sealed envelope placed on the inside back-cover of the textbook; perhaps a CD-ROM that a student could use to do accounting homework). Second, many publishers "bundled" a printed course review book (perhaps a review of chapters and key terms in an art history textbook) with the printed book to be used by a student; course review books were almost always enclosed in a durable plastic wrap with the textbook. Third, all of the publishers eventually launched online learning management systems (LMSs; e.g., a password protected online system containing, perhaps, mathematics homework or quizzes, etc.), and students paid (perhaps between $50.00 and $100.00) to the publisher or the bookstore to access the LMS. Of course, faculty members had to be convinced that every student must participate in an LMS. Fourth, a few publishers began releasing a small cluster of digital e-textbooks at high prices.

Ironically, the publishers received rather interesting responses to their LMS offerings; many students complained about having to pay to take a chapter quiz. These early digital textbooks generated few positive responses from students. Clearly, increases in suggested prices were the only viable strategy for the five largest publishers to generate more revenues and profits. This turned out to be a fundamentally flawed strategy. The publishers effectively committed the marketing errors highlighted by Levitt. They were product (i.e., textbook) and not market (i.e., student) oriented, and the student market for new textbooks was undergoing substantive changes, triggered by major, and, in many ways, unprecedented, technological changes that challenged ultimately the textbook publisher's basic business model.

We know from various consumer behavior studies that many consumers tend to survey the marketplace to find the best price for a product, and according to the National Association of College Stores (NACS) data in Table 2.6, students are consumers. By 2010, only 31% of college students purchased a new printed textbook; 32% purchased a used printed book; 16% of the students rented the book; and 10% of students never obtained any textbook. Some students borrowed a copy of the book (8%), used a copy from the college library (2%), and a very small number rented an e-textbook (1%). Table 2.6 has the data.

Table 2.6 Where college students obtained or purchased college textbooks: 2010

Purchased new printed textbooks	31%
Purchased used printed textbooks	32%
Rented printed textbooks	16%
Never obtained a required textbook	10%
Borrowed textbook from friend or classmate	8%
Used library copies	2%
Rented electronic e-textbook	1%

Source: National Association of College Stores (NACS), *The College Store Magazine*, May–June 2010, pp. 17–20. Student Monitor

THE BACKLASH AGAINST COLLEGE TEXTBOOK PRICES

Clearly, students, many faculty members, a growing number of members of the U.S. Congress, as well as a vocal cluster of public interest non-governmental organizations (NGOs) were not happy about what they perceived to be "rapacious" new textbook price increases. Textbook prices and widely popular digital technologies triggered a transformation in the U.S. textbook marketplace. New online companies emerged to satisfy the needs of college students looking for lower textbook prices, often available at less than 50% of a new book's SRP on some websites.

The entrepreneurs at the popular secondary market online operations, including the well-established Amazon and eBay, realized that new, used, and rented college textbooks were durable products (i.e., a durable product with a "normal wear and tear" had a usable life-span of at least 3 years; examples of durable products include refrigerators, washing machines, etc.). This understanding of student behavior caught the attention of a number of scholars, including Judith Chevalier, and Austan Goolsbee in a well-received working paper.[15] There was also an outpouring of scholarly articles and NGO reports, which were covered extensively by newspapers and magazines, concerned about the prices of new textbook editions.[16]

CONCLUSION

Things fall apart; the centre cannot hold...
William Butler Yeats "The Second Coming"[17]

Between 2001 and 2012, the major textbook publishing firms were whipsawed by the impact of disruptive technologies, two recessions, student and faculty negative responses to high prices, online sites selling used and rental textbooks, and academic libraries placing some textbooks on reserve. Some faculty members eschewed textbooks relying instead on case studies, articles, PowerPoint slides, and hand-outs. The self-publishing of textbooks by faculty members started to gain traction in the college market.

However, the emergence of online book piracy sites, copyright infringement issues, concerns about academics posting copyrighted materials online, and the importation of textbooks from foreign markets (some of which were pirated versions) posed even more serious, long-term threats to the beleaguered U.S. textbook industry's basic business model. Frustrated by these intellectual property issues, the textbook industry sought to use the legal protections in the U.S. copyright law (i.e., 17 U.S.C.) to seek remedies in federal courts. They spent hundreds of thousands of U.S. dollars in legal fees in their quest to tamper down and ultimately destroy what they perceived to be a direct assault on their legal properties, their "castles." Unfortunately, not all of their litigation was successful, and this situation would dominate the years between 2000 and 2021 and well beyond 2021.

Notes

1. L. (Yogi) Berra. "20 Great Yogi Berra quotes," www.authenticmanhood.com/blog/20-great-yogi-berra-quotes.
2. National Bureau of Economic Research (NBER). "U.S. Business Cycle Expansions and Contractions," www.nber.org/research/data/us-business-cycle-expansions-and-contractions. The following quote is the NBER's definition of a recession. "A recession is a significant decline in economic activity spread across the economy, lasting more than a few months, normally visible in real GDP, real income, employment, industrial production, and wholesale-retail sales. A recession begins just after the economy reaches a peak of activity and ends as the economy reaches its trough. Between trough and peak, the economy is in an expansion. Expansion is the normal state of the economy; most recessions are brief, and they have been rare in recent decades."
3. The Internet Society. "Brief History of the Internet," www.internetsociety.org/internet/history-internet/brief-history-internet.
4. R. Spector. *Get Big Fast: Inside the Revolutionary Business Model That Changed the World* (New York: Harper Business, 2000), pages 1–88. Also

see G.L. Stigler. "The Economies of Scale," *The Journal of Law and Economics*, 1 (October 1958), 54–71.

5. Google. "From the Garage to the Googleplex," https://about.google/intl/en_US/our-story. Also see J. Valinsky, I. Sherman. "Google's Incredible Growth: A Timeline;" www.cnn.com/interactive/2018/12/business/google-history-timeline.

6. Statista. "Sales of Tablets and iPads in the U.S. from 2010 to 2012," www.statista.com/statistics/271942/sales-of-tablets-and-ipads-in-the-us-until-2012/#:~:text=In%202010%2C%209%2C7%20million,including%208%2C8%20million%20iPads. Also see F. Benhamou. "Fair Use and Fair Competition for Digitized Cultural Goods: The Case for e-Books," *Journal of Cultural Economics*, 39, 1 (2015): 123–131.

7. T.H. Grubesic, E.A. Mack. *Broadband Telecommunications and Regional Development* (London: Routledge, 2016), pages 46–95.

8. Statista. "Number of Smartphones Sold to End Users Worldwide from 2007 to 2020," www.statista.com/statistics/263437/global-smartphone-sales-to-end-users-since-2007.

9. U.S. Department of Commerce. Bureau of the Census. *Statistical Abstract of the United States 2012*. Section 12. Labor Force, Employment, & Earnings, www2.census.gov/library/publications/2011/compendia/statab/131ed/tables/labor.pdf.

10. E. Brynjolfsson, M.D. Smith. "Frictionless Commerce? A Comparison of Internet and Conventional Retailers," *Management Science*, 46, 4(April 2000), 563–585.

11. C.M. Christensen. *The Innovator's Dilemma: The Revolutionary Book That Will Change the Way You Do Business* (New York: Harper Business, 2011), *page xv*.

12. *Ibid.*, pages xviii and xxvii–xxix.

13. E. Truelove, L.A. Hill, E. Tedards, "Kathy Fish at Proctor and Gamble: Navigating Industry Disruption by Disrupting from Within," Harvard Business School Case 421-012, July 2020. Also see T. Nicholas. "How History Shaped the Innovator's Dilemma," Harvard Business School Working Paper 21-014.

14. J. Lepore. "The Disruption Machine: What the Gospel of Innovation Gets Wrong," *The New Yorker*, www.newyorker.com/magazine/2014/06/23/the-disruption-machine.

15. J. Chevalier, A. Goolsbee. "Are Durable Goods Consumer Forward Looking? Evidence from College Textbooks," National Bureau of Economic Research Working Paper 11421, www.nber.org/papers/w11421. Also see S. Yin, R. Saibal, H. Gurnani, A. Animesh. "Durable Products with Multiple Used Goods Market: Product Upgrade," *Marketing Science*, 29, 3 (May/June 2010), 840–560, 580. M. Waldman.

"Durable Goods Theory for Real World Markets," *Journal of Economic Perspectives, 12*, 1 (Winter 2003), 131–154.

16. H.L. Roediger. "Why Are Textbooks So Expensive?" Association for Psychological Science, https://web.archive.org/web/20180317041203. Also see C. McFadden. "Are Textbooks Dead? Making Sense of the Digital Transition," *Publishing Research Quarterly, 28*, 2 (2012), 93–99. N.H. Nicholls. "The Investigation Into the Rising Cost of Textbooks," www.lib.umich.edu/files/SPOTTextbookBackground.pdf. D. Merriman. "Do Textbook Publishers Release New Editions Too Frequently?" www.doi.org/10.2139/ssrn.579401. K. Molina. "Digital Asset Pricing in the Textbook Market," www.doi.org/10.2139/ssrn.1868262. Student PIRG. "Ripoff 101," https://studentpirgs.org/2005/02/27/ripoff-101-2nd-edition. M.G. Watt. "Research on the Textbook Publishing Industry in the United States of America," https://files.eric.ed.gov/fulltext/ED498713.pdf. T. Lizuka. "An Empirical Analysis of Planned Obsolescence," *Journal of Economics & Management Strategy, 16*, 1 (Spring 2007), 191–226. J. Hechinger. "As Textbooks Go 'Custom, Students Pay," *The Wall Street Journal,* www.wsj.com/srticles/SB121565135185141235. T. Lewin. "Students Find $100 Textbooks Cost $50, Purchased Overseas," *The New York Times,* www.nytimes.com/2003/10/21/us/students-find-100-textbooks-cost-50-purchased-overseas.html. J. Milliot. "B & N College Expands Textbook Rental Program." *Publishers Weekly,* https://www.publishersweekly.com/pw/by-topic/industry-news/bookselling/article/44104-b-n-college-expands-textbook-rental-program.html. J. Rosen. "College Bookstores in Dynamic Times." *Publishers Weekly,* https://www.publishersweekly.com/pw/by-topic/industry-news/bookselling/article/48981-college=bookstores-in-dynamic-times.html.

17. W. B. Yeats. "The Second Coming," https://poets.org/poem/second-coming.

CHAPTER 3

The Responses of the Major College Textbook Publishers: 2013–2018

Abstract By 2013, college bookstores reported sales declines. And there was and growing acceptance by college students of relying on Amazon.com, Abe.com, and other online websites as an important and growing source of textbooks. These websites accounted for an estimated market share of about 54% of total college textbook sales. Unfortunately, 2014 was the highpoint in new textbook revenues. The results for the years after 2014 were, at best, unsettling to the textbook publishers. New textbook sales revenues declined to −16.55% between 2013 and 2018. The Consumer Price Index (CPI) increased to +11.80% between 2013 (an index of 233.0) and 2018 (251.1; +7.77%). This compelled publishers to review and ultimately consider changing or modifying their business models. In addition, copyright infringement cases emerged, and the Kirtsaeng decision, which reached the Supreme Court of the U.S., was a serious blow to the traditional textbook strategy of limiting the importation of certain legally printed and published college textbooks into the U.S. The online textbook websites benefited significantly from this decision because they could offer new legally printed and published textbooks from foreign markets at lower prices than the comparable new text costs in the U.S.

Keywords Textbook categories • College bookstores • U.S. Copyright Law • Copyright infringement cases

© The Author(s), under exclusive license to Springer Nature   33
Switzerland AG 2023
A. N. Greco, *The College Textbook Publishing Industry in the
U.S. 2000–2022*, Marketing and Communication in Higher
Education, https://doi.org/10.1007/978-3-031-30415-6_3

SOME POSITIVE BUSINESS DEVELOPMENTS IN 2013

By 2013, there were a few, but unfortunately not many, positive indicators in the higher education new textbook sector. First, there was some financial stability in the sale of new textbooks in the top ten textbook book categories, including (1) psychology posted $285 million in new textbook sales; (2) foreign languages and literature, $234 million; (3) biological sciences (non-majors), $209 million; (4) biological sciences (majors), $209 million; (5) computers and information systems, $197 million; (6) chemistry, $175 million; (7) mathematics, $161 million; (8) English composition and rhetoric, $152 million; (9) English composition-handbooks, $142 million; and (10) interdisciplinary studies-college orientation, $132 million.

Second, many of these very successful textbook categories also recorded the lowest rates of used textbook sales (e.g., mathematics, 18% used sales; biological sciences, 17%; foreign language and literatures, 14%; and chemistry 13%). Third, an analysis of textbook ISBN numbers (ISBN, the International Standard Book Number; every book has a unique numerical book identifier number and either a 13-digit or a 16-digit code and a bar code; ISBN was introduced in 1970) revealed strong annual sales of a cluster of new titles including *The Art of Public Speaking*, $96 million in sales; *The Publication Manual of the American Psychological Association*, $90 million; and *Campbell's Biology*, $84 million. However, declines were posted in what had been reliably profitable textbook categories (e.g., marketing, legal studies, geography, linguistics, library and information sciences, architecture).[1]

UNSETTLING DATA

We Here Are On The Wrong Side of the Tapestry
G.K. Chesterton in *The Innocence of Father Brown*[2]

However, publishers became very concerned when the detailed 2014 NACS data revealed that traditional college bookstore chains in the U.S. (e.g., Barnes & Noble Education, Follett Corporation, etc.) accounted for only 23% of new textbook sales in the previous year. Augmenting their concern was the fact that textbook sales at the large chain bookstores stood at only 11%. Small retail stores near colleges generated about 12% of text sales.[3]

So, it was apparent that among an increasing number of students, there was a wide and growing acceptance of eschewing the traditional retail outlets for textbooks and relying instead on Amazon.com, Abe.com, and other online websites as an important if not the major source of textbooks. These websites accounted for an estimated staggering market share of about 54% of total college textbook sales. Amazon.com had a large 38% market share of text sales, and other online sites (e.g., E-Bay) accounted for 16%. If this were not bad enough, the NACS data indicated that used textbook sales in 2013 topped 7 million units generating $266 million in sales, an increase of +90% over 2012. Academic fields with high used book rates included dance at 48%; anthropology, history, and philosophy, all were at the 47% level; and sociology, classics, theater, parks and recreation, art, and criminal justice posted 45% rates. The largest rental disciplines included English, psychology, mathematics, history, and biological sciences. Ironically, there were a few academic areas with rather low used printed textbook sales, and they included nursing and engineering at 21% (i.e., many scientific textbooks incorporated new research findings thereby limiting the usefulness of an older text) and accounting at 17%[4] (possibly because of annual accounting changes issued by the Financial Accounting Standards Board (FASB; an important non-profit board that establishes and improves the Generally Accepted Accounting Principles, GAAP, for the accounting profession in the U.S.)).

Other substantive business problems included sharp declines in expensive hardcover textbook sales (accounting for approximately 25% of all higher education book sales); steep increases in the sale of less expensive paperback textbooks (reaching the 60% threshold). In addition, the publishers were concerned about uneven "sell-through" rates for new textbooks, including English and American literature, with a 40% sell-through; economics, 29%; mathematics and statistics, 32%; and psychology, 28%. Compounding these developments was an increased demand for custom textbooks ($167 million in sales revenues in 2013), and these books posted an impressive 23% market share. Sell-through rates for these texts were intriguing, including 73% in English; 50% in both economics and mathematics; and 44% in psychology. Other major concerns included a –2.69% decline in student enrollments between

2013 and 2018; and Table 3.1 has the enrollment details. And the unnerving fact is that many enrolled students failed to buy the required textbook (e.g., in the English text sector, 40% of college students did not purchase a required text; mathematics stood at a 32% rate; economics at 29%; and psychology with only 28%). Ironically, the available data revealed a phenomenal demand for used textbooks but a paltry demand for the rentals of new texts in 2013. The rentals of English and American literature book were a small 6.15%, computers and information sciences books posted an even smaller 5.28% rate, marketing rentals barely "moved the needle" at 2.1%, quantitative business fields (e.g., economics; finance) hovered at 1.87%, and film/cinema studies was a small 1.53%.[5]

Yet another substantive problem for publishers was the emergence of viable self-publishing textbook companies. These firms offered an author expertise in all aspects of the publishing process, and most authors lacked any substantive knowledge about editorial, art, design, page make-up, lithographic (sometimes called litho, offset, and photo-offset) printing (most textbooks were printed using the litho process because of its speed and economics), paper, binding processes, digital e-book procedures, indexing, and so on. Other important self-publishing considerations for an academic author included attractive royalty rates (some paid a 70%

Table 3.1 Total U.S. non-profit public and private college students: 2013–2018

Year	Undergraduate and graduate students			Total annual percentage change
	Full-time	Part-time	Total	
2013	12,596,610	7,780,067	20,376,677	−1.30%
2014	12,454,464	7,754,628	20,209,092	−0.82%
2015	12,287,512	7,700,692	19,988,204	−1.09%
2016	12,125,314	7,721,590	19,846,904	−0.71%
2017	12,077,304	7,688,294	19,765,598	−0.41%
2018	12,103,000	7,725,000	19,828,000	−0.32%
Percent change 2013–2018	−3.92%	+0.71%	−2.69%	+0.32%

U.S. Department of Education. National Center for Education Statistics, https://nces.ed.gov/programs/digest/d18/tables/dt18_303.10.asp

N.B. All numbers were rounded off and may not always equal 100%

royalty versus about 10% from the big textbook publishers) and low used book sales since the text could be "updated" annually. In addition, many of these firms offered very competitive book prices (some self-published textbooks in 2013 and in the following years had prices that started at $39.95), and most self-publishing operations offered both print and a digital text bundles, frequently at $49.95. Other important business features included prompt communications with authors and business stability. The author wrote the book, and a company handled all of the back office, sales, distribution, revenue collection, and royalty operations.

Textbook Publishers Confront "Sisyphus"[6]

Textbook publishers believed they had to raise new book prices to compensate for lackluster sales performances. According to data released by the NACS, between the academic years 2012–2013 and 2013–2014, the average new hardcover and paperback textbook SRP increased +9.72%. This trend continued into the 2014–2015 academic year (+3.8%) and in 2016–2017 (+12.5%). The average costs for used textbooks during those same years remained well below the price for new texts, allowing student to spend fewer dollars on educational materials. In fact, NACS reported that "average" student textbook expenditures declined to –6.45% between 2012 and 2013 (which stood at $682) and 2013–2014 ($638), and other steep declines of –11.76% were posted between 2013–2014 and 2014–2015 ($602). This downward trend was also evident in subsequent academic years: 2016–2017 ($576) and 2017–2018 ($484).[7]

Publishers also realized that any textbook price change, even small ones, had the potential to impact big events in their revenues.[8] Between 2012 and 2013, new textbook revenues, according to the Association of American Publishers (AAP), increased slightly from $4.29 billion to $4.34 billion (+1.17%). The Consumer Price Index (CPI) datasets, released by the Federal Reserve Bank of Minneapolis, increased to +1.48%, and this index indicated increased costs in the U.S. for various products (e.g., paper, ink, and binding), many of which impacted textbook publishers' unit manufacturing costs. However, price increases for new textbooks surged +11.75% between 2013 and 2014 (reaching $4.85 billion in net publishers' revenues).

Unfortunately, 2014 was the highpoint in new textbook revenues. The results for the years after 2014 were, at best, unsettling to textbook publishers. New textbook sales revenues declined a horrific –16.55% between

2013 and 2018. The Consumer Price Index (CPI) increased to +11.80% between 2013 (an index of 233.0) and 2018 (251.1; +7.77%). This conundrum compelled publishers to review and ultimately consider changes or modifications to their business models. Table 3.2 has the details.

In addition, competition for student's textbook dollars accelerated. Amazon.com offered college students a free six-month trial for Amazon Prime, and after the end of the trial, the annual subscription was about $59. Amazon Prime offered students exclusive offers including (generally) free shipping for college textbooks and a student membership in Grubhub, and deep discounts were available for Apple Music Unlimited and the popular Prime Video channels, all for $1 per month, and so on. A growing number of colleges had Amazon lockers, with direct Amazon deliveries for students, on campuses, and this accelerated Amazon.com's business among college students for textbooks and other consumer products. Since many families had an Amazon Prime subscription, there was no cost to a student if he or she used the parent's account for campus deliveries of textbooks and other products.[9]

Another very successful educational competitor in the college textbook sector was Chegg Inc. (which stood for "chicken and egg"). Chegg offered students a wide array of higher educational products, including

Table 3.2 U.S. net college new textbook revenues: 2013–2018 ($ billions), and the Consumer Price Index (CPI): 2013–2018

Year	New textbook revenues	Consumer Price Index (CPI)
2013	$4.34	233.0
2014	$4.85	236.7
2015	$4.53	237.0
2016	$3.96	240.0
2017	$3.98	245.1
2018	$3.62	251.1

Source: The Association of American Publishers (AAP). Also see AAP datasets in Publishers Weekly, various issues. *The Bowker Annual* and *The Library and Book Trade Almanac*, various years. The Federal Reserve Bank of Minneapolis. The Consumer Price Index (CPI). Base year 1982–1984 = 100. N.B. All numbers were rounded off and may not always equal 100%

www.minneapolisfed.org/about-us/monetary-policy/inflation-calculator/consumer-price-index-1913 renting and selling printed texts and e-textbooks; it also offered "textbook solutions" (which Chegg described as a "step-by-step explanations for thousands of textbooks"). In addition, Chegg offered students access to its library of more than 30 million homework solutions, practice quizzes, guided videos, and math solvers.[10]

BookScouter.com emerged with an incredibly easy-to-use app and website. Once the app was downloaded, a student, using a smart phone or a tablet, for example, scanned or typed the textbook's ISBN to determine the best new, used, or rental price from more than 30 online vendors. BookScouter.com provided a printed address label for a student selling, for example, a copy of a music history textbook, and payment for the sale of a student's textbook was remarkably accurate and fast. BookScouter.com bypassed effectively Amazon, the other online sites, and the college bookstore, making it easy for a student to buy, sell, or rent a textbook.[11]

Unfortunately, not every online site selling or renting textbooks complied with the U.S. Copyright Law, and websites selling illegal educational products were sued in the Southern District of New York (SDNY) for copyright infringement. All of the major textbook publishing firms provided instructors with ancillary materials. For example, Prentice Hall maintained a website for +1500 college textbooks including Kotler-Armstrong's *Principles of Marketing* textbook, one of the U.S.'s bestselling introductory marketing books. Prentice Hall (which is part of Pearson PLC) offered a secure site that required a faculty member to be "cleared" (i.e., verified that the individual was a faculty member at a college) to access and use the materials on the website. Once a faculty member had access, he or she could order a copy of the book, and the faculty member could read and download (into an MS Word document) the entire book's copyrighted chapter outlines and multiple-choice questions and answers for each chapter. In addition, complete access to the text's PowerPoint slides were available. A number of websites, possibly more than 230 according to the legal documents submitted to the Southern District of New York (SDNY), offered for sale a text's multiple-choice questions and answers for every chapter in the textbook. A review of several of these websites revealed that multiple-choice questions and answers for all 20 chapters in Kotler-Armstrong's *Principles of Marketing* and all 14 chapters in Solomon's *Consumer Behavior* textbooks (also a very successful Prentice Hall textbook) were available for sale. The Kotler-Armstrong tests and answers cost approximately $22; the Solomon test questions and answers were available for about $35. A review of the websites listed in the litigation revealed that test questions and answers were available for college textbooks published by Cengage, McGraw-Hill, John Wiley, Macmillan, and other publishers. Since this litigation was not settled when this book was printed, detailed information about the plaintiffs and defendants was excluded from this book.[12]

The Search for Clarity and Certainty

Since the dawn of time, business executives have despised uncertainty, which is precisely what textbook publishers confronted after 2013. Data for the years 2013–2018 on the humanities, the social sciences, and the science and technology textbook categories indicated that textbook publishers released 10,399 new titles in the humanities (and SRP's increased to +4.23% between 2013 and 2018), averaging an impressive 1733 new books published annually. The social sciences' total results (15,736 new books and 2622 annually) clearly were significant. Average annual SRPs declined a modest –1.1% during those years. The highly publicized science and technology (STM) sector released only 6844 new titles (hovering at the 1090 average annual new title output level), and the average SRPs sustained a –7.29% decline. Table 3.3 has the details.

In the important English and American literature category, with 1928 new titles (and an annual new book output of almost 321 titles), average suggested retail prices increased to +8.99% between 2013 and 2018. North American history sustained a –13.81% decline in average textbook

Table 3.3 Average suggested retail prices (SRPs) and new title output for new hardcover and paperback U.S. college textbook revenues in the humanities, the social sciences, and science and technology: 2013–2018 (U.S. dollars)

Year	Humanities SRP (new units)	Social sciences SRP (new units)	Science and technology SRP (new units)
2013	$70.53 (2009)	$68.03 (2945)	$70.27 (1155)
2014	$71.35 (2146)	$68.19 (2886)	$69.20 (1222)
2015	$69.05 (1903)	$70.05 (2758)	$70.11 (1162)
2016	$72.53 (1594)	$68.12 (2528)	$75.90 (913)
2017	$71.20 (1435)	$66.58 (2313)	$71.36 (1206)
2018	$73.51 (1312)	$67.28 (2306)	$65.15 (887)

Source: *The Bowker Annual* and *The Library and Book Trade Almanac*, various years. N.B. The number in the parentheses is new title output. These are average prices for hardcover and paperback textbooks. The average price for a hardcover text is higher than the cost for a paperback title

Table 3.4 Average suggested retail prices (SRPs) and new title output for new hardcover and paperback U.S. college textbook revenues in English and American literature, North American history, and chemistry: 2013–2018 (U.S. dollars)

Year	English and American literature SRP (new units)	North American history SRP (new units)	Chemistry SRP (new units)
2013	$72.45 (547)	$63.37 (349)	$107.12 (21)
2014	$69.18 (365)	$49.60 (441)	$86.65 (36)
2015	$67.34 (326)	$50.10 (397)	$73.31 (30)
2016	$73.29 (283)	$51.15 (386)	$105.31 (27)
2017	$69.06 (206)	$50.33 (335)	$121.51 (29)
2018	$78.96 (201)	$54.62 (343)	$101.78 (21)

Source: *The Bowker Annual* and *The Library and Book Trade Almanac*, various years. N.B. The number in the parentheses is new title output. The average prices for hardcover and paperback textbooks. The average price for a hardcover text is higher than the cost for a paperback title

prices, releasing 2251 new books (averaging annually slightly more than 375 titles). Chemistry's record was not as dramatic, dropping –4.99% in average SRPs, with only 164 new titles during those years (and a very modest 25 new texts annually). Table 3.4 has the details.

Net publisher revenues in 2018 ($3.62 billion), as indicated in Table 3.2, were lower than in 2013 ($4.34 billion; –$720 million between 2013 and 2018) in spite of the fact that the Consumer Price Index (CPI) increased to +7.77% during those years, and publishers raised annually the suggested retail prices of texts. These trends compelled executives again to reevaluate all of their traditional business and marketing practices.

THE IMPORTANCE OF INTELLECTUAL PROPERTY TO COLLEGE TEXTBOOK PUBLISHERS

Ever since 1790, book publishers have been strong supporters of the First Amendment of the U.S. Constitution which created legal protection for intellectual property (IP). IP consists of patents, trademarks, and copyright. While some publishers had an intrinsic interest in trademarks (e.g., *Penguin* books) and patents (especially publishers that had sophisticated pre-press, printing, and binding operations; e.g., Bertelsmann AG), copyrights were of upmost importance to every publisher since it was the "fuel" that supported and protected a book's copyright.

The legal foundation for intellectual property in the United States is Article 1 § 8 of the U.S. Constitution. "The Congress shall have power to... promote the progress of science and useful arts, by securing for limited times to authors and inventors the exclusive right to their respective writings and discoveries..."[13] The First Amendment of the U.S. Constitution, part of the "Bill of Rights," does not address specifically intellectual property; however, it does deal with ideas and concepts of great importance to book publishers. "Congress shall make no law respecting an establishment of religion, or prohibiting the free exercise thereof; or abridging the freedom of speech, or of the press; or the right of the people peaceably to assemble, and to petition the government for a redress of grievances."[14]

Article 1 § 8 and the First Amendment are both rather brief. Therefore, it was up to the Congress of the United States to draft and pass laws designed specifically to offer protection for patents, trademarks, and copyrights. So, the responsibility to write and pass a copyright law fell onto the shoulders of the new Congress, and they passed the first copyright law in 1790, based essentially on England's 1710 copyright law. In the following decades, the Congress updated infrequently the copyright law in 1831, 1870, 1909, 1976, and 1998.[15]

Today, the Copyright Law of the U.S. is found in 17 U.S.C., which is approximately a 480-page law that described in detail the terms and conditions of copyright in this nation. The chapter numbers and topics that impact textbooks include Chapter 1: Subject Matter and Scope of Copyright; Chapter 2: Copyright Ownership and Transfer; Chapter 3: Duration of Copyright; Chapter 4: Copyright Notice, Deposit, and Registration; Chapter 5: Copyright Infringement and Remedies; Chapter 6: Importation and Exportation; and Chapter 7: Copyright Office.[16]

Fortunately, the U.S. Copyright Office (which is part of the Library of Congress) prepared a series of circulars to provide relevant copyright information to non-legal specialists. What follows are excerpts from relevant Copyright Office's circulars that provide an overview of some, but clearly not all, of the substantive issues contained in 17 U.S.C.

"Copyright Basics, Circular 1" defined copyright as "a form of protection provided by the laws of the United States to the authors of 'original works of authorship' that are fixed in a tangible form of expression. An original work of authorship is a work that is independently created by a human author and possesses at least some minimal degree of creativity. A work is 'fixed' when it is captured (either by or under the authority of an author) in a sufficiently permanent medium such that the work can be perceived, reproduced, or communicated for more than a short time. Copyright protection in the United States exists automatically from the moment the original work of authorship is fixed... Copyright provides the owner of copyright with the exclusive right to: reproduce the work in copies...; prepare derivative works based upon the work; distribute copies... of the work to the public by sale or other transfer of ownership or by rental, lease, or lending... Copyright also provides the owner of copyright the right to authorize others to exercise these exclusive rights, subject to certain statutory limitations...."

Ironically, "copyright does not protect: ideas, procedures, methods, systems, processes, concepts, principles, or discoveries; works that are not fixed in a tangible form...; titles, names, short phrases, and slogans; familiar symbols or designs... In general, for works created on or after January 1, 1978, the term of copyright is the life of the author plus 70 years after the author's death. If the work is a joint work with multiple authors, the term lasts for 70 years after the last surviving author's death. For works made for hire and anonymous or pseudonymous works, the duration of copyright is 95 years from publication or 120 years from creation, whichever is shorter... For works created before January 1, 1978, that were published or registered before that date, the initial term of copyright was 28 years from the date of publication with notice or from the date of registration. At the end of the initial term, the copyright could be renewed for another 67 years for a total term of protection of up to ninety-five years..."[17]

Circular 21's "Reproduction of Copyrighted Works by Educators and Librarians" addressed the complex and often confusing issue of "fair use" by college professors. "The provisions make certain uses of copyrighted works permissible without first obtaining permission of the copyright owner. One of the most discussed of these statutory provisions is known as 'fair use,' a legal doctrine that promotes freedom of expression by permitting the unlicensed use of copyright-protected works in certain circumstances... Section 107 of the Copyright Act provided the statutory framework for determining whether something is a fair use and identifies certain types of uses—such as criticism, comment, news reporting, teaching, scholarship, and research—as examples of activities that may qualify as fair use. Section 107 calls for consideration of the following 4 factors in evaluating a question of fair use. Purpose and character of the use, including whether the use is of a commercial nature or is for nonprofit educational purposes: Courts look at how the party claiming fair use is using the copyrighted work, and are more likely to find that nonprofit educational and noncommercial uses are fair. This does not mean, however, that all nonprofit education and noncommercial uses are fair, and all commercial uses are not fair; instead, courts will balance the purpose and character of the use against the other factors below. Additionally, 'transformative' uses are more likely to be considered fair. Transformative uses are those that add something new, with a further purpose or different character, and do not substitute for the original use of the work... Nature of the copyrighted work: This factor analyzes the degree to which the work that was used relates to copyright's purpose of encouraging creative expression. Thus, using a more creative or imaginative work is less likely to support a claim of a fair use than using a factual work (such as a technical article or news item). In addition, use of an unpublished work is less likely to be considered fair. Amount and substantiality of the portion used in relation to the copyrighted work as a whole: Under this factor, courts look at both the quantity and quality of the copyrighted material that was used. If the use includes a large portion of the copyrighted work, fair use is less likely to be found; if the use employs only a small amount of copyrighted material, fair use is more likely. That said, some courts have found use of an entire work to be fair under certain circumstances. And in other contexts, using even a small amount of a copyrighted work was determined not to be fair because the selection was an important part—or the 'heart'—of the work. Effect of the use upon the potential market for or value of the copyrighted work: Here, courts review whether, and to what extent, the unlicensed use harms the existing or future market for the copyright owner's original work. In assessing this factor, courts consider whether the use is hurting the current market for the original work (for example, by displacing sales of the original) and/or whether the use could cause substantial harm if it were to become widespread... Courts evaluate fair use claims on a case-by-case basis, and the outcome of any given case depends on a fact-specific inquiry. This means that there is no formula to ensure that a predetermined percentage or amount of a work—or specific number of words, lines, pages, copies—may be used without permission..."[18]

IMPORTANT COLLEGE TEXTBOOK COPYRIGHT CASES: KIRTSAENG V. JOHN WILEY

There have been a number of significant copyright cases since 1790.[19] However, several important cases since 2000 highlighted the critical importance of copyright to authors and publishers, including the entire college textbook sector. The Kirtsaeng decision by the Supreme Court of the United States, which upended the Bobbs-Merrill Co. v. Straus decision in 1908,[20] was arguably the most important textbook copyright case in the first two decades of this century.

Supap Kirtsaeng was a graduate student studying in the U.S., and he was concerned about the prices he paid for his textbooks. He realized that the average cost of a specific textbook in his native Thailand was lower than the SRP for that same textbook in the U.S. So, he asked relatives to purchase legally textbooks in Thailand and send them to Supap in the U.S. Kirtsaeng then posted these textbooks on an online site(s) to sell them to students in the U.S. In essence, Kirtsaeng utilized the basic financial concept of arbitrage. Andrei Shleifer and Robert W. Vishny wrote that arbitrage was "the simultaneous purchase and sale of the same, or essentially similar, security in two different markets for advantageously different prices.. Even the simplest realistic arbitrages are more complex than the textbook definition suggests..."[21] Since the dawn of time, merchants have used arbitrage. For example, in ancient Rome a merchant might buy grain from a farmer, and the merchant could then sell the grain at a profit to a consumer interested in making bread. Today, a supermarket buys milk from a manufacturer or a distributor (in a business-to-business transaction; known as B-2-B in marketing) and then sells the milk to a consumer (in a business-to-consumer transaction; B-2-C) who needs milk for breakfast. In essence, Kirtsaeng discovered an inefficiency in the textbook market between a specific textbook's SRP in Thailand and Trenton, NJ.

John Wiley sued Kirtsaeng in the Southern District of New York (SDNY) in 2008; while it was never made clear, Wiley argued that Kirtsaeng's arbitrage might have earned him more than $1 million.[22] However, the fundamental legal issue stipulated in Wiley's lawsuit centered on the important "First Sale Doctrine" since Wiley assigned "to its wholly owned foreign subsidiary (i.e., Wiley Asia) rights to publish, print, and sell foreign editions of Wiley's English language textbooks abroad. Wiley Asia's books state that they are not to be taken (without permission) into the United States."[23] Wiley argued that Kirtsaeng did not have the legal authority to import any book(s) into the U.S. that had the above restriction. The United States Department of Justice (DOJ) has commented on the "First Sale Doctrine." "Few issues have created greater confusion in criminal copyright prosecutions than the 'First Sale Doctrine.' The doctrine is one of the specific statutory restrictions which Congress has placed on the exclusive rights of copyright owners. Criminal defendants frequently resist prosecution by claiming that they believed that the works they were selling had been the subject of a legitimate first sale..."[24]

The "First Sale Doctrine" was addressed by the Supreme Court of the United States in the landmark Bobbs-Merrill Co. v. Straus case. The Supreme Court's decision in that case was as follows. "The complainant in the circuit court, appellant here, the Bobbs-Merrill Company, brought suit against the respondents, appellees here, Isidor Straus and Nathan Straus, partners as R. H. Macy & Company, in the circuit court of the United States for the Southern District of New York (SDNY), to restrain the sale of a copyrighted novel, entitled 'The Castaway,' at retail at less than $1 for each copy. The circuit court dismissed the bill on final hearing: 139 Fed. 155. The decree of the circuit court was affirmed on appeal by the circuit court of appeals: 77 C. C. A. 607, 147 Fed. 15. The appellant is the owner of the copyright upon 'The Castaway,' obtained on the 18th day of May 1904, in conformity to the copyright statutes of the United States. Printed immediately below the copyright notice, on the page in the book following the title page, is inserted the following notice: 'The price of this book at retail is $1 net. No dealer is licensed to sell it at a less price, and a sale at a less price will be treated as an infringement of the copyright'."[25] Based on the historic Bobbs-Merrill decision, Kirtsaeng lost in the Southern District of New York. He appealed to the Second Circuit. Again, Wiley prevailed.[26] As a last resort, Kirtsaeng appealed to the Supreme Court, which agreed to hear the appeal.

The Supreme Court ruled in a 6-3 decision against Wiley's defense of the "First Sale Doctrine" and the language in 17 U.S. C. §106(3).[27] Justice Breyer wrote the majority opinion, and he stated the following. "Wiley published Walker's *Fundamentals of Physics, 8th ed.* through the Wiley Asia operation. This foreign version contained the following statement: 'Copyright © 2008 John Wiley & Sons (Asia) Pte. Ltd. All rights reserved. This book is authorized for sale in Europe, Asia, Africa, and the Middle East only; and may not be exported out of these territories. Exportation from or importation of this book to another region without the Publisher's authorization is illegal and is a violation of the Publisher's rights. The Publisher may take legal action to enforce its rights... Printed in Asia.'"[28]

Justice Breyer pointed out that "we must decide whether the words 'lawfully made under this title' restrict the scope of §109(a)'s 'first sale' doctrine geographically.' However, Kirtsaeng insisted that the words 'lawfully made under this title' as imposing a non-geographical limitation. He says they mean made 'in accordance with' or 'in compliance with' the Copyright Act."[29]

Justice Breyer listed a series of major concerns, which he called the "horribles," that he felt could threaten certain segments of society. "Associations of libraries, used book dealers, technology companies, consumer-goods retailers, and museums point to various ways in which a geographical interpretation would fail to further basic constitutional copyright objectives... The American Library Association tells us that library collections contain at least 200 million books published abroad (presumably, many were first published in one of the nearly 180 copyright-treaty nations and enjoy American copyright protection under 17 U.S.C. §104)... and that a geographical interpretation will likely require the libraries to obtain permission (or at least create significant uncertainty) before circulating or otherwise distributing these books..."[30] Justice Breyer also mentioned that "during 2000–2009 a significant amount of book printing moved to foreign nations."[31]

Justice Breyer's majority opinion stated that "In Kirtsaeng v. John Wiley & Sons, Inc., 568 U. S., this Court held that petitioner Supap Kirtsaeng could invoke the Copyright Act's 'first-sale doctrine,' see 17 U. S. C. §109(a), as a defense to the copyright infringement claim filed by textbook publisher John Wiley & Sons, Inc."[32]

CONCLUSION

This decision was a serious blow to the traditional textbook strategy of limiting the importation of certain legally printed and published college textbooks into the U.S. The online textbook websites, on the other hand, benefited significantly from this decision because they could now offer new legally printed and published textbooks from various foreign markets at lower, and in some instances significantly lower, SRPs than the comparable new text costs in the U.S.

Notes

1. Nielsen Pub Track Higher Education. "The U.S. College Textbook Market," www.slideshare.net/bisg/carl-kulo-pub-track-for-higher-education-2014.
2. G.K. Chesterton. *The Innocence of Father Brown* (New York: Sterling Publishing, 2005), pp. 56–57.
3. National Association of College Stores (NACS). www.nacs.org/advocacynewsmedia/pressreleases/tabid/1579/ArticleID/939/NACS-Report-Student-Spending-on-Course-Materials-Continues-to-Decline.aspx. NACS has approximately 4000 college bookstore members. Also see Association of American Publishers (AAP), "Student spending on college course materials continues multi-year decline," www.publishers.org/news/student-on-college-course-materials-continues-multi-year-decline.
4. National Association of College Stores. "NACS Report Shows 14 Percent Decrease in Spending on College Course Materials," www.nacs.org/nacs-report-shows-14-decrease-in-spending-on-college=course-materials.
5. *Ibid.* Also see A. Rowe. "College Students Spent 23 Percent Less on Textbooks in Fall 2019," www.forbes.com/sites/adamrowe1/2019/12/13/college-students-spent-23-less-on-textbooks-in-fall-2019/#2fbdb23b589d. Also see *Publishers Weekly.* "B & N College Expands Textbook Rental Program," https://www.publishersweekly.com/pw/by-topic/industry-news/bookselling/article/44104-b-n-college-expands-textbook-rental-program.html. R. Deahl. "More College Stores Renting Textbooks," https://www.publishersweekly.com/pw/by-topic/industry-news/bookselling/article/45813-more-college-stores-renting-textbooks.html. J. Rosen. "The College Bookstore Disrupted," https://www.publishersweekly.com/pw/by-topic/industry-news/bookselling/article/72133-the-college-bookstore-disrupted.html. J. Milliot. "B & N Grapples with Changing College Market," https://www.publishersweekly.com/pw/by-topic/industry-news/financial-reporting/article/80565-b-n-education-grapples-with-changing-college-market.html.
6. A. Camus (author), J. O'Connor (translator). *The Myth of Sisyphus and Other Essays* (New York: Vintage, 2018), 119–123. Sisyphus, in Greek mythology, was condemned to push a large boulder up a mountain, only to see it roll down again.
7. National Association of College Stores. www.nacs.org/advocacynewsmedia/pressreleases/tabid/1579/ArticleID/939/NACS-Report-Student-Spending-on-Course-Materials-Continues-to-Decline.aspx. Also see J. Rosen. Rethinking College Stores. *Publishers Weekly,* https://

www.publishersweekly.com/pw/by-topic/industry-news/bookselling/
article/76150-rethinking-college-stores.html.

8. I. Newton. "Newton's Third Law of Motion," www.grc.nasa.gov/
WWW/K-12/airplane/newton.html. "The third law states that for every
action (force) in nature there is an equal and opposite reaction. In other
words, if object A exerts a force on object B, then object B also exerts an
equal force on object A..." Also see D. Sharma. "Complexity Economics,"
The Economics Review, https://theeconreview.com/2019/01/30/
complexity-economics. D. Levy. "Chaos Theory and Strategy: Theory,
Application, and Managerial Implications," *Strategic Management Journal*,
15, 1(1994), 167–178. C.A. Hidalgo. "Economic Complexity Theory and
Applications," *Nature Reviews Physics* (2021); https://doi.org/10.1038/
s42254-020-00275-1. C. Oestreicher. "A History of Chaos Theory,"
Dialogues in Clinical Neuroscience, 9, 3(September 2007): 279–289. "The
smallest of changes in a system can result in very large differences in that
system's behavior." J.L. Vernon. "Understanding the Butterfly Effect,"
The American Scientist, 105, 3(May-June 2017), 130. C. Werndl. "What
Are the New Implications of Chaos for Unpredictability," *The British
Journal for the Philosophy of Science*, 60, 1(2009), 195–220. A. Hubler.
"Adaptive Control of Chaotic Systems," *Swiss Physical Society, Helvetica
Physica Acta*, 62(1989), 339–342.

9. Amazon.com. "Start Your [Prime] 6-Month Trial," www.amazon.
com/amazonprime?_encoding=UTF8&_bncoding=UTF8&hvadi
d=381655816708&hvdev=c&hvdvcmdl=&hvexid=&hvlocint=&h
vlocphy=9003627&hvnetw=g&hvpone=&hvpos=&hvptwo=&hvq
mt=b&hvrand=1336767733848927623&hvtargid=kwd-3320874
03556&planOptimizationId=WLPStudentMonthlyEligiblePlans&p
rimeCampaignId=studentWlpPrimeRedir&primeCampaignIdPref=
studentWlpPrimeRedir&ref=pd_sl_6e5rr9bsw_b&ref_=st_wlp_pr_
redir&tag=googhydr-20. Also see Amazon Textbook Rentals, www.
amazon.com/rentals/b/ref=ps20_ben_tr/?node=17853655011.
Amazon. "Amazon Prime Student Discount," www.businessinsider.com/
amazom-prime-student-discount-2021.

10. Chegg. "About Us," www.chegg.com.

11. Bookscouter.com. "BookScouter Helps You Sell Textbooks and Used
Books for the Most Money by Comparing Offers from Over 30 Book
Buyback Vendors with a Single Search," www.bookscouter.com. Some of
the other online platform sites buying textbooks include Cash4Books;
Student2Student, Decluter; BookRun; eCampus; BookFinder; etc.

12. The websites analyzed were involved in litigation in the Southern District
of New York (SDNY) when this book was printed. The allegations presented by the Educational Publishers Enforcement Group (EPEG)

involved possible violation(s) of the U.S. Copyright Law regarding the selling of textbook test answers and/or solution manuals. Since this matter was not resolved when this book was printed, the name(s) and the email(s) of the defendants and/or firms were not listed.

13. U.S. Constitution. "Article 1 §8," www.archives.gov/founding-docs/constitution-transcripts.

14. U.S. Copyright Office. "Copyright Law of the United States and Related Laws Contained in Title 17 of the United States Code," www.copyright.gov/title17/title17.pdf.

15. *Ibid.*

16. Ibid. Also see Greco. "The Kirtsaeng and Sci-Hub Cases: The Major U.S. Copyright Cases in the Twenty-First Century," *Publishing Research Quarterly,* 33, 3(September 2017), 238–253. J.D. Litman. "Copyright, Compromise, and Legislative History," *Cornell Law Review* 72, 5 (1987), 857–904. N. Elkin-Koren. "The Changing Nature of Books and the Uneasy Case for Copyright," https://papers.ssrn.com/sol3/cf_dev/AbsByAuth.cfm?per_id=2783962. U.S. Copyright Office. "Circulars," www.copyright.gov/circs. O.F. Afori. "The Evolution of Copyright Law and Inductive Speculations as to its Future," *Journal of Intellectual Property Law,* 19, 2(2012), 253–259. M. O'Hare. "Copyright and the Protection of Economic Rights." *Journal of Cultural Economics,* 6,1 (1982): 33–48.

17. U.S. Copyright Office. "Copyright basics: Circular 1," www.copyright.gov/circs/circ01.pdf.

18. U.S. Copyright Office. "Reproduction of Copyrighted Works by Educators and Librarians, Circular 21," www.copyright.gov/circs/circ21.pdf.

19. W.S. Strong. *The Copyright Book: A Practical Guide, 6th ed.* (Cambridge: MIT Press, 2014), 56–77. Also see B.F. Marks. "Copyright Protection, Privacy Rights, and the Fair Use Doctrine: The Post-Salinger Decade Reconsidered," *New York University Law Review,* www.nyulawreview.org/wp-content/uploads/2018/08/NYULawReview-72-6-Marks.pdf. S. Asokan. "Demystifying the Honest Infringer: Reorienting Our Approach to Online Copyright Infringement Using Behavioral Economics," *Journal of Intellectual Property & Practice,* 13, 9 (September 2018), 729–743.

20. Supreme Court of the United States. "Syllabus Kirtsaeng, dba Bluechristine99 *v.* John Wiley & Sons, Inc. certiorari to the United States Court of Appeals for the Second Circuit No. 11-697. Argued October 29, 2012—Decided March 19, 2013," www.supremecourt.gov/opinions/12pdf/11-697_4g15.pdf.

21. A. Shleifer, R.W. Vishny. "The Limits of Arbitrage," *The Journal of Finance,* LII, 1(March 1997), 35–56.

22. United States District Court Southern District of New York (SDNY). "John Wiley & Sons, Inc. v. Supap Kirtsaeng D/B/A/ Bluechristine 99 and John Doe Nos. 1–5," www.pacermonitor.com/view/B7QIENA/ John_Wiley_&_Sons_Inc_v_Supap_Kirtsaeng_et_al__nysdce-08-07834 __0001.0.pdf.
23. Supreme Court of the United States. "Kirtsaeng, dba Bluechristine99 v. John Wiley & Sons, Inc."
24. United States Department of Justice. "Copyright Infringement— First Sale Doctrine," www.justice.gov/archives/jm/criminal-resource-manual-1954-copyright-infringement-first-sale-doctribe.
25. Bobbs-Merrill Co. v. Straus, 210 U.S. 339 (1908), https://supreme.justia.com/cases/federal/us/210/339. United States Supreme Court. "No. 176. Argued: Decided: June 1, 1908." Also see P.H. Lim. "Copyright in Logos and Exhaustion of Rights Under the First Sale Doctrine in Grey Markets," *Journal of Intellectual Property Law & Practice*, 7, 9 (September 2012), 663–672.
26. United States Court of Appeals, Second Circuit. "John Wiley & Sons, Inc. Plaintiff-Appellee v. Supap Kirtsaeng D/B/A/ Bluechristine 99 Defendant-Appellee. Argued: May 19, 2010. Decided: August 15, 2011," www.legale.com/decision/infco20110815074.
27. Supreme Court of the United States. "Kirtsaeng, dba Bluechristine99 v. John Wiley & Sons, Inc."
28. *Ibid.*
29. *Ibid.*
30. *Ibid.*
31. *Ibid.* This is a reference to Albert N. Greco. "Global Recession Dampens U.S. Book Exports and Imports in 2009," in D. Bogart (ed.), *Library and Book Trade Almanac 2010: 55th ed.* (Medford, NJ: Information Today, Inc., 2010), pp. 499–522.
32. Supreme Court of the United States. "Kirtsaeng, dba Bluechristine99 v. John Wiley & Sons, Inc." Also see E. Rosati. "U.S. Supreme Court Holds First Sale Doctrine Applicable to Works Lawfully Made Abroad," *Journal of Intellectual Property Law & Practice*, 8, 8 (August 2013), 590–591. I. Reimers. "Can Private Copyright Protection Be Effective? Evidence from Book Publishing," *Journal of Law and Economics*, 59, 2 (May 2016), 411–440. C.D. Asay. "Kirtsaeng and the First Sale Doctrine's Digital Problem," www.stanfordlawreview.org/online/kirtsaeng-and-the-first-sale-doctrines-digital-problem/#footnote_1.

CHAPTER 4

College Bookstores and College Textbook Publishers Confront Dramatic Developments and Challenges: 2019–2021

Abstract By 2019, it was clear that the "Big 5" college textbook publishers were unable to implement new effective marketing strategies and structures to address the insidious problems undermining their basic business model: student enrollment increases were small; in 2021, net publisher revenues declined to only $3.22 billion, –0.62% from $3.24 billion in 2000; the Open Access (OA) and the Open Educational Resource (OER) free textbook sectors posted impressive increases between 2019 and 2021; in 2020, most colleges went remote utilizing online instruction, which had a deleterious impact on textbook sales through the Summer of 2021; and many students moved from print and relied instead on e-textbook rentals, reaching 15% in 2020 and topping 31% in 2021; potential mergers in the textbook industry; and the inevitable search for "scale." The "Big 5" developed some innovative strategies, but too many of them faltered.

Keywords College bookstores • The ReDigi case • Txtbook revenue • Open Access • Open Education Resource • Covid pandemic • Digital textbooks • P & L • Inclusive Access • Antitrust Litigation

THE STATE OF COLLEGE TEXTBOOK PUBLISHING IN 2019–2021

By 2019–2021, most of the major textbook companies realized, albeit reluctantly, that they had failed to understand completely the changing textbook marketplace, and by 2019, it was clear that they were unable to implement new and effective marketing strategies and structures to address the problems undermining their basic business model.

Their numerous basic problems included the following. First, total full-time and part-time undergraduate and graduate student enrollment was at best anemic for 2019, and the data for 2021–2021 was equally underwhelming. So, the total 3-year growth rate was a paltry +0.26%. Table 4.1 has the data. Second, new textbook revenue trends were also troubling. Revenues stood at $3.30 billion in 2019 and only $3.13 billion in 2020 (down –5.15% from the previous year) and posting $3.22 billion in 2021 (–2.42% between 2019 and 2021). In Table 2.2, 2000 net textbook revenues were $3.24 billion; so, the publishers recorded an unsettling –0.62% decline between 2000 and 2021. The Consumer Price Index (172.2 in 2000; it was 271.0 in 2021) surged +57.38% during those years. Table 4.2 has the details.

Third, members of Congress of the U.S. introduced legislation in 2019 to "expand the use of [free] open textbooks in order to achieve savings for students and improve textbook price information…"[1] If such legislation passed and became law, the Open Access (OA) and the Open Educational

Table 4.1 Total U.S. non-profit public and private college students, 2019–2021

Year	Undergraduate and graduate students			Total annual percentage change
	Full-time	Part-time	Total	
2019	12,135,000	7,768,000	19,904,000	+0.38%
2020	12,133,000	7,795,000	19,928,000	+0.12%
2021	12,129,000	7,828,000	19,956,000	+0.14%
Percent change 2019–2021	+0.05%	+0.77%	+0.26%	–

Source: U.S. Department of Education. National Center for Education Statistics, https://nces.ed.gov/programs/digest/d18/tables/dt18_303.10.asp

N.B. All numbers rounded off and may not always equal 100%

Table 4.2 U.S. net college new textbook revenues, 2019–2021 ($ billions), and the Consumer Price Index (CPI), 2019–2021

Year	New textbook revenues	Consumer Price Index (CPI)
2019	$3.30	255.7
2020	$3.13	260.5
2021	$3.22	271.0
Percent change 2019–2021	–2.42%	+5.98%

Source: The Association of American Publishers (AAP). Publishers Weekly; https://www.publishersweekly.com/pw/by-topic/industry-news/publisher-news/article/90440-2021-was-stellar-year-for-publishing.html. Also see AAP datasets in Publishers Weekly, various issues. *The Bowker Annual* and *The Library and Book Trade Almanac*, various years. The Federal Reserve Bank of Minneapolis. The Consumer Price Index (CPI). Base year 1982–1984 = 100. N.B. All numbers rounded off and may not always equal 100%

www.minneapolisfed.org/about-us/monetary-policy/inflation-calculator/consumer-price-index-1913

Resource (OER) free textbook sector could grow and impact negatively all of the college textbook publishers. For example, OpenStax was an impressive OER operation, and in 2019, OpenStax textbooks were used by more than 2.2 million students, which effectively posed a serious financial risk to the "Big 5" publishers.[2]

Fourth, the impact of the Covid-19 pandemic impacted everyone in the U.S. (and abroad), almost every U.S. college and college bookstore closed, and classes were transferred to online (e.g., Zoom) teaching. The impact on the college textbook sector was alarming. Closed colleges meant closed college bookstores, and Barnes & Noble Education (BNED) reported devastating college store financial loses. By March 2020, BNED released documents indicating consolidated third quarter sales were $502.3 million, down –8.3% reflecting higher education's rapid evolution to digital courseware.[3] In April 2020, the company sent out emails to students recommending that they use the B & N college store website to order digital books for Spring and Summer 2020 semesters, and a large percentage of the company's bookstore employees were furloughed.[4] In July 2020, BNED reported that their most recent sales were only $256.9 million, down –23.2% from the same quarter in 2019. In September 2020, BNED's financial results were equally unsettling: revenues of only $204 million, down –36.2% since "fewer students at college campuses have limited the sales of textbooks and also pressured the broader retail segment" of insignia products (e.g., tee-shirts, jackets, coffee mugs, NACS reported that the profit margin for insignia products was generally 50% versus about 23% for new textbooks, and the "average" margin for used textbooks was about 35%). By December 2020, B & N still had some closed college stores and experienced continued depressed sales.[5]

Fifth, by 2020, what type of textbook was utilized, and where it was obtained, changed significantly from the 2010 NACS data (see Table 2.6). Textbooks have three selling seasons: the fall semester (the most important one for unit and sales revenues); the spring semester, generally smaller than the fall semester, but still exceptionally important; and the summer, while important, is very small. Industry executives were convinced that textbook sales were (using a textbook industry phrase) "baked in" for the Spring 2020 semester since students obtained a text at the start of the spring semester, probably sometime in January for semester courses and March for colleges on a quarter system. Most colleges did not close and go exclusively online until sometime in mid-March 2020. However, the NACS and AAP data marked a dramatic and essentially an unusual shift from 2010. The percentage of students using new printed textbooks was 31% in 2010, and in 2020, it topped 42%. Unfortunately, NACS did not provide any reason(s) for this rather dramatic shift toward new printed textbooks. The purchase of used printed textbooks declined from 32% in 2010 to 20% in 2020 (again, a rather unusual shift in student purchasing patterns), and this decline was balanced by the fact that the number of students renting and using an e-textbook grew from 1% in 2010 to 15% in 2020. The 2021 NACS results were not complete. However, new purchased printed text sales in 2021 sagged to 32% from 42% in 2020, used text tallies increased modestly to 22% (from 20%), and renting printed textbooks data hovered at the 15% level (down from 19%). However, the rental rate for a limited e-textbook (probably for only for 1 semester or 1 academic quarter) was a dramatic 31% (up sharply from 2020's 6%). Unfortunately, the 2021 NACS data was not available for the unlimited renting of e-textbooks, or the total number of students who never purchased a text shared with a friend or used a library copy. Table 4.3 has the 2020 and the preliminary 2021 details.

Why did these very unusual changes occur in 2020 and especially in 2021? Were they just the result of the Covid lockdown and the widely publicized movement toward online classes that took place in the U.S. starting sometime in March 2020? Or were the changes impacted by

Table 4.3 Where college students purchased or obtained college textbooks: 2020–2021

Category	2020	2021
Purchased new printed textbooks	42%	32%
Purchased used printed textbook	20%	22%
Rented printed textbook	19%	15%
Rented e-textbook (unlimited use)	9%	N/A
Rented e-textbook (limited use)	6%	31%
Never obtained the textbook, or borrowed a copy from a friend, classmate, or from the library	4%	N/A

Source: National Association of College Stores. Student Monitor. Association of American Publishers (AAP), https://vimeo.com/432496326. Also see S. Jaschik. "Student Spending on Course Materials Fell 22% in 2021-2022," https://www.insidehighered.com/quicktakes/2022/05/18/student-spending-course-materials-fell-22-2021-2022. Association of American Publishers (AAP). "A Victory for Affordability: Student Spending on Course Materials Declined 22% During the 2021-2022 Academic Year," https://www.publishers.org/news/%ef%bf%bca-victory-for-affordability-student-spending-on-course-materials-declines-22-during-the-2021-2022-academic-year. N.B.: The data for 2021 is preliminary and not complete. AAP will release revised statistics sometime in the last half of 2022

increases in the growth of streaming services of music (e.g., Spotify) and filmed entertainment (e.g., Netflix) by students during the Covid lockdown? Were 2020 and 2021 "unique years" with exceptional but transitory developments? Or were the results a harbinger of future trends? Or were there other reasons for these trends? Clearly, additional research studies with access to more data, after 2021, are needed to ascertain more precisely the initial short-term and long-term implications of the wider acceptance by students of e-textbooks in 2020 and 2021.

The Impact on the "Big 5" College Textbook Publishers

The "Big 5" publishers also confronted the impact of this unparalleled Covid pandemic. All of the "Big 5" textbook publisher's offices were closed. Employees in editorial, sales, production, and so on worked remotely (except for the textbook warehouse personnel), and this trend continued into 2021 and 2022. At least one textbook publisher announced that remote work would continue into mid-to-late 2023, and there has been reports that employees of editorial, sales, and so on might continue to work remotely for the "foreseeable future."

Textbook revenues cratered. Bloomberg reported that "this year [2020], it looks more likely it'll just be a breaking point."[6] Pearson was perhaps better positioned than many of the other "Big 5" to withstand this unnerving pandemic with its 42.7% market share of the higher education textbook sector (before the U.S. colleges closed in March 2020) and its financial reserves. However, Pearson's revenues for the first half of 2020 were down –17% from the previous year. Pearson's U.S. textbook sector experienced "print declines and modest digital growth, [with] uncertainty on college enrollments..." John Fallon announced his retirement, and Pearson hired Andy Bird, a former international executive with the Walt Disney Company, to replace Fallon.[7]

Cengage's financial results were also unsettling. Revenues in early 2020 were down –6%, and the company's declines continued, –7% by June 2020, and –17% by the first quarter of 2021 (i.e., the fall 2020 semester).[8] McGraw-Hill, reeling from its failure to merge with Cengage, reported that textbook revenues were down –12.44%, and print sales were off –63% in 2020. In April 2020, Fitch Ratings "reaffirmed the Long-Term Issuer Default Rating (IDR) of McGraw-Hill Global Education Holdings, LLC (MHGE) and McGraw-Hill Global Education Finance, Inc. (MHGE Finance) at B+. A financial rating of B+ is a non-investment grade credit rating used by Moody's, Standard & Poor's (S&P), and Fitch (three major U.S. financial ratings companies) for an issued debt instrument (generally a bond) or the issuer of the credit (i.e., company or business)." McGraw-Hill announced in December 2020 that it had "entered into a transaction support agreement to address (i.e., to refinance) its near-term debt maturities."[9]

John Wiley, a diversified publishing company with trade and professional book units and an extensive, very successful, and impressive scholarly journal operation (especially in the STM sector which generated cash because of annual or multi-year journal subscription revenues), posted strong results in March and June and equally impressive results in November 2020. They reported that they saw substantial benefits in the shift from print to digital trade, textbooks, and especially in the scholarly journal sector. Macmillan Learning, part of a global publishing corporation, did not report textbook financial results since the tallies were incorporated into its trade book operations.[10]

Sixth, while the suggested retail prices (SRPs) for texts in the humanities, the social sciences, and the science and technology fields all increased, new title output declined in the humanities and the eclectic STM sectors, and they increased slightly in the social sciences, hardly encouraging results. Table 4.4 has the details.

Table 4.4 Average suggested retail prices (SRPs) and new title output for new hardcover and paperback U.S. college textbook revenues in the humanities, the social sciences, and science and technology: 2019–2021 (U.S. dollars)

Year	Humanities SRP (new units)	Social sciences SRP (new units)	Science and technology SRP (new units)
2019	$76.90 (1438)	$66.73 (1860)	$67.83 (1041)
2020	$78.81 (1015)	$78.56 (1741)	$95.09 (627)
2021	$84.26 (1146)	$84.47 (1855)	$101.31 (512)
Percent Change	+9.57% (−20.31%)	+26.58% (+0.27%)	+49.36% (−50.82%)

Source: American Library Association. "Prices of U.S. Published Materials," https://alair.ala.org/handle/11213/14600

Table 4.5 Average suggested retail prices (SRPs) and new title output for hardcover and paperback U.S. college textbook revenues in English and American literature, North American history, and chemistry: 2019–2021 (U.S. dollars)

Year	English and American literature SRP (new units)	North American history SRP (new units)	Chemistry SRP (new units)
2019	$80.68 (227)	$48.96 (245)	$102.74 (13)
2020	$80.17 (167)	$58.60 (184)	$141.21 (12)
2021	$80.65 (181)	$55.86 (201)	$152.56 (17)
Percent change 2019–2021	−0.04% (−20.26%)	+14.09% (−17.96%)	+48.49% (+30.77%)

Source: American Library Association. "Prices of U.S. Published Materials," https://alair.ala.org/handle/11213/14600. N.B. Before 2013, this data was listed in *The Library and Book Trade Almanac*

This trend was also evident between 2019 and 2021 in three major textbook categories: English and American literature had negative tallies for suggested retail prices in these 3 years, −0.04%, and new title output was −20.26%. North American history's prices during those same years increased a hefty +14.09%; unfortunately, new title output dropped a sharp −17.96%. Chemistry's data was impressive with a +48.49% surge in suggested retail prices and +30.77% in new title output, albeit on a very small number of new titles. Table 4.5 has the details.

The Impact on College Bookstores

While most of this data was troubling, detailed studies for 2019–2021 released by the NACS did not brighten the outlook of textbook publishers or college bookstores. Some of NACS' key findings for these years included the following: student use of digital materials increased significantly to +26% between 2019 and 2020, and this trend continued into 2021; NACS assumed this trend would continue in 2022 and the years after 2022. Yet far too many students (+25%) failed to obtain course materials.

As if these trends were not sufficiently upsetting, NACS reported that 49% of all college faculty members did not require any educational course material for at least one of their courses, and an additional 10% of the surveyed faculty members did not require any educational materials for their students. In 2021, NACS revealed that while 78% of college students at NACS member college bookstores purchased or acquired course materials, 32% (i.e., of the 78% of college students in the NACS dataset) purchased new printed texts, 31% relied on used printed textbooks, 35% rented, and 30% downloaded materials for free.[11]

Textbook Publishers Adopted Innovative Marketing Theories to New Business Conditions

The end result was that almost every textbook publishing corporation, trying to understand the complex, shifting sands of the marketplace, decided to craft an intriguing, eclectic variety of new business marketing strategies including evaluating the growing acceptance of e-texts; understanding more precisely the nature of the financial risk in publishing new textbooks that did not have strong sell-through rates; addressing the company's scale, that is having effective economies of scale and mass production, to grow the business enterprise, as well as distribution strategies, and creating more effective entry barriers (specifically a stronger "moat") to combat the used and rental markets.[12]

Augmenting these concerns was a "growing" acceptance by publishers and editors of the basic strategic and marketing ideas developed by Michael Porter. In essence, they accepted the fact that they had failed to implement some of Porter's substantive theses before the Covid pandemic's impact on their sales. This meant that most of the textbook publishing houses had to consider developing more effective financial controls to insure that the firm had, or had access to, enough capital (known in financial circles as having enough "dry power") to pay for current and future business opportunities; releasing more digital textbooks while decreasing (and eventually eliminating) printed only texts; implementing clear and effective strategies and structures that stressed managing for the long term rather than concentrating only on short-term goals; and crafting a "disintermediation" strategy (i.e., a "direct-to-consumer," D-2-C), and this meant selling print or digital textbooks directly to students, increasing profit margins, bypassing a reliance on college bookstores, and avoiding the traditional "23%" discount rate offered by publishers to the bookstores. Lastly, Porter's theories meant using strategies to minimize and ultimately "destroy" the entire used and rental online business and address effectively the intense criticism of textbook suggested retail prices as well as the important and growing open access (OA) and open educational resource (OER) movement.[13]

W. Chan Kim and Renee Mauborgne built on Porter's intellectual framework when they developed an innovative "Blue Ocean" marketing and financial strategy. "Blue Ocean" was designed to divide an existing market, in this case college textbooks, into new sectors for opportunities and financial growth. That is, to "fish" or sell in "blue" waters with few if any competitors and not in hotly contested "red" waters (i.e., textbook categories filled with too many competitors). In essence, this meant thinking outside the box, evaluating existing products and services, and ascertaining what competitive advantages the firm had and which ones could it develop. The desired end result was to make competitors irrelevant.[14]

While the "Big 5" higher education textbook publishing firms considered a wide variety of innovative strategies, far too many of the strategies were, in reality, just words written on an office whiteboard, on a computer screen, and on printed strategy documents. These words had to be turned into effective business plans in the highly competitive U.S. textbook sector with the appropriate financial and human resources and the correct "marketing mix," that is, the "4Ps" (product, price, placement, and promotion) as well as the "5th P" (i.e., purchasing) to address the numerous problems plaguing the industry and to rejuvenate some lackluster product lines.

THE SEARCH FOR SCALE: PLAN A

You're gonna need a bigger boat.
Roy Scheider in *Jaws*[15]

In light of the herculean challenges confronting textbook publishers, and their rather slow decisions to modify their marketing strategies, Cengage and McGraw-Hill decided in 2019 to merge; the goal was to gain scale, to become "bigger" in the sector, to have a "bigger boat" of products and services than any of their college textbook competitors. This merger was subject to U.S. Government approval because of the nation's antitrust laws (specifically the Sherman Antitrust Act of 1890 and the Clayton Antitrust Act of 1914).[16] The rationale presented by McGraw-Hill for the merger was intriguing. "Together, we will usher in an era in which all students can afford the quality learning materials needed to succeed—regardless of their socioeconomic status or the institution they attend. Additionally, the combined company will have robust financial strength to invest in next-generation products, technology and services that create superior experiences and value for millions of students."[17]

However, in spite of their efforts to convince U.S. Government antitrust regulators that this merger would not violate the nation's antitrust laws and impact adversely consumers (i.e., students) and textbook prices, intense opposition to this merger emerged. And the parties were compelled to abandon their plans, which was a significant set-back for both companies.[18]

THE SEARCH FOR SCALE: PLAN B

It became clear after the announcement and failure of the Cengage-McGraw-Hill merger that the other "Big 5" textbook publishers also needed a "bigger boat" if they were to remain viable business enterprises in an industry that posted declining annual net revenues. This prompted the other college textbook publishing firms, perhaps reluctantly in some cases, to develop and accept some new, innovative business marketing strategies, many of which had been proposed originally by Ted Levitt and Michael E. Porter. One intriguing approach, adopted by most of the publishers, involved launching textbook rental options. Ironically, while the publishers were drafting various rental strategies, the two largest college bookstore chains (Barnes & Noble Education and Follett) moved faster and rather efficiently into this enterprising business opportunity.

Follett, with about 850 college stores, announced they were developing a "pilot" rental program in Michigan and California. "The stores will offer about 20% of their titles for rent, charging 42.5% of the [suggested retail] purchase price..." Follett later broadened the pilot for all of its college bookstores. Barnes & Noble Education (BNED) college stores also announced a program for their 624 stores "renting books at 35% of the [suggested retail] list price..." B & N and Follett, for example, acquired "used" textbooks several different ways. First, they bought books from students (called "buy backs" in the business) in their college stores at the end of a semester. Second, they had access to used books from various distributors including the successful MBS Textbook Exchange (MBS) which supplied books to more than 700 college bookstores, stocked more than 150,000 titles, and shipped more than 10 million books annually. In 2017 MBS was acquired by BNED for $174.2 million. Third, there was a network of independent entrepreneurs that visited colleges and purchased textbooks directly from college professors, paying cash at the time of the sale, and they sold these texts to one of the national chains or to distributors. Fourth, an added incentive was The Higher Education Opportunity Act of 2008 which "included $10 million for grants to support textbook rental pilot programs... [and] more than 20 college bookstores have applied for grants."[19]

Cengage, McGraw-Hill, Pearson, and the other publishers, all late to the rental textbook business, announced plans to launch their own rental programs. "Cengage's rental program will begin with several hundred titles this year... McGraw-Hill is taking a different route into rentals, through a partnership with Chegg, a fast-growing online textbook rental business...McGraw-Hill will supply 25 of its books to Chegg in return for a portion of the rental revenue..." These publisher rental programs were a good start, but they were rather limited in both the scope and the breadth of their rental offerings. "Students who choose Cengage's rental option will get immediate access to the first chapter of their book electronically, in e-book format, and will have a choice of shipping options for the printed book..."[20]

The college bookstore chains, with direct and daily access to a large captive audience of students on their college campuses, posted some impressive results with their innovative rental programs. For example, at a growing number of college bookstores, if a student picked up a new copy of a textbook and brought it to the cash register (called "cash wrap" in the business) to pay for the book, the clerk at the cash register asked a student if he or she wanted to buy or rent the textbook, effectively and efficiently creating an immediate rental business without having a cluster of used textbooks on the shelf.

However, Cengage, McGraw-Hill, Pearson, and the other publishing firms were disappointed with the lackluster response to their rental initiatives. So, the publishers slowly revised their rental programs. One interesting approach was the "Cengage Unlimited" strategy, which was highly touted by the publisher in press releases and during conference calls with financial service analysts. In this "unlimited" program, a student paid a flat fee and had access to all of Cengage's textbooks. This worked if a student had more than one class that required a Cengage textbook; otherwise, it was economically unprofitable to a student. Ultimately, Cengage and the other publishers were unable to replicate the highly popular rental programs from Amazon and the other online sites or the direct student contact offered by employees in a college bookstore.[21]

Compounding the problem in launching rentals was the fact that Cengage and McGraw-Hill were viewed as companies in a state of "transition." Cengage had filed for bankruptcy under Chapter 11 on July 2, 2013, which had tarnished its reputation in the financial service sector, and Cengage was dependent on working with financial companies for capital. Chapter 11's bankruptcy law stipulates that a firm can reorganize a debtor's business affairs, debts, and assets. Cengage emerged from bankruptcy on April 1, 2014, eliminating approximately $4 billion of its funded debt and securing $1.75 billion in exit financing.[22] In 2012, McGraw-Hill sold its educational publishing operation to Apollo Global Management (APO); the selling price was not disclosed.[23] Apollo Global Management, Inc., is a "global alternative investment manager firm. Founded in 1990, Apollo is a high-growth, global alternative asset manager with a focus on: yield, hybrid and equity." In 2021, Apollo (APO) had $498 billion in assets under management (i.e., AUM); this AUM tally increased to $512.8 billion in March 2022.[24]

Pearson, at the time it decided to create a superb rental program, essentially had the financial and operational resources, and the market position and scale, to address the rental option in a bigger and more successful way than some of its competitors. Pearson PLC (PSO) is a public corporation with corporate headquarters in the U.K. and major offices in the U.S. In 2013, John Fallon replaced the exceptionally successful CEO Marjorie

Scardino (an American woman from Texas who won the Pulitzer Prize in newspaper journalism before she was hired by Pearson). So, in 2013, Pearson's Prentice Hall (Pearson's textbook operating unit) was the largest, most successful textbook publisher in the U.S. with a "good" financial foundation, a broad portfolio of operating units, and, arguably, a superb sales force calling on faculty members.

Pearson's major rental program, after several years of intense planning, was launched in cooperation with the National Association of College Stores (NACS has about 4000 college bookstore members). Pearson's strategy was designed to undermine, and hopefully take business and revenues away from, the online and college bookstore rental book business. If printed texts were only available for a rental fee and not sold, then the inventory of used books sold by retailers would disappear in about 3–5 years. The terms and conditions of their rental program meant that every Pearson printed textbook would be distributed via a consignment model. In the U.S., the vast majority of all books were sold on consignment to bookstores and other retailers. The rental procedure was fairly straight forward. Participating college bookstores ordered and obtained rental units, and they reported the rental transactions to Pearson. A textbook(s) was rented to a student for 1 semester or academic quarter, and the student was required to return the book(s) at the end of the term, at which point the book was again rented to another student for 1 term, and so on. Hardcover printed textbooks were durable products, and, assuming normal wear and tear, a hardcover textbook could be rented on average between five and possibly seven times. Students who did not return the book(s) at the end of the term were charged a non-return fee and possibly the cost of the book. The college bookstore had access to the student's college identification information, making late charges or charging the student for the price of the textbook generally possible. If a specific title was not requested by a faculty member, or if the sell-through rate was lower than anticipated, the book(s) was either returned by the bookstore to Pearson or disposed of in accordance with Pearson's instructions (e.g., in case the book was damaged beyond use). The bookstore could also "sell" access codes for Pearson's Learning Management Systems (LMS; an online service that offered students review material, weekly quizzes or tests, etc.). A college would determine if a student's financial aid could be used to rent a textbook(s). Eventually, most of the other major textbook publishers adopted rental programs with terms and conditions that "mirrored" essentially those announced and implemented by Pearson.[25]

However, the tide turned eventually against Pearson. First, Pearson was primarily a printed textbook company with a remarkably small number of digital books. This fact was of concern to financial analysts in the U.K. and in the U.S. as well as Pearson's stockholders (e.g., US Bankcorp, Deutsche Bank, Morgan Stanley, Credit Suisse, etc.). Second, the years between 2014 and 2017 were difficult ones for Pearson, and the company's steep decline in profits after 2017 were clearly a warning sign to Fallon and to the financial service sector of stock analysts that followed or invested in Pearson. Under Fallon, Pearson sold a number of assets to generate the cash needed to convert its large and impressive printed book operations into a diversified digital strategic business unit (i.e., an SBU), including in 2015, the sale of *The Financial Times* and *The Economist,* and in 2017 two partial shares in the legendary and immensely successful and well-respected Penguin Books, a trade book publisher with more than 3000 titles in its famed Penguin Classics book series, to Bertelsmann AG (the publisher of Random House, an exceptionally large trade book company). The remaining third and final portion of Penguin Books was sold to Bertelsmann in 2020 (and Bertelsmann renamed the new entity Penguin Random House; PRH). This transaction cleared the antitrust regulatory review in the U.S. and in the E.U.[26] Its unsettling financial situation compelled Pearson to get a "bigger boat" than any of its competitors, and this meant crafting a bold, innovative, long-term digital strategy. The sale of assets provided Pearson with most of the necessary finances required to undertake what was a tremendous reconfiguration of Pearson's higher education SBUs from a print orientation to a primary digital publishing operation.

The essential points of Pearson's digital marketing strategy included expanding its share of the higher education textbook market through the development of a substantive digital transformation called "Digital First," which included a mix of digital textbooks, Learning Management Systems, and user-friendly content platforms. The "Digital First" strategy was a substantive shift from publishing and selling printed textbooks to retailers to the publishing, ownership of, and controlling student access to the digital content of its more than 1500 college textbook titles. The company's rationale was addressed in its 2020 trading update. "Campus bookstores are buying less physical inventory due to changing student behavior with over 50% of learners now preferring an e-book to a physical text. This is shown in good e-book growth. Both these trends provide more affordable options for students giving them less reason to turn to the secondary market and over time will increasingly create a more predictable, visible revenue stream…"[27] Pearson spent more than $70 million creating digital files for many of their existing and new textbooks. Coverage of the "Digital First" strategy was extensive. *Publishers Weekly* reported that "Pearson will move all of its 1500 U.S. textbook titles to continuously updated digital content and make print textbooks available only on a rental basis."[28]

The next phase in Pearson's strategy was to rent only digital textbooks and to "exit" slowly but inevitably from the printed book world. Their rationale was clear: profit margins were better in a non-print higher education textbook marketplace.[29] However, Pearson believed it was now ready to roll out a complete direct-to-consumer (D-2-C) program to students.

In 2020, the last part of Pearson's "Digital First" strategy was launched. It was a D-2-C option. This allowed the company to publish, own (a key strategic idea), and distribute its digital content. The decision to develop a D-2-C program took a great deal of planning and financing. Pearson reported that its "digital and digitally enabled" course materials was 59% in 2017, growing to 62% in 2018, and slightly more than 66% in 2019. This transformation enabled Pearson to reduce print sales and increase digital sales and profits. Pearson reported that it sold 21 million printed college textbooks in 2010. The growing availability of "digital and digitally enabled" course materials helped Pearson to decrease print sales: in 2016, the company sold 7.4 million printed texts; in 2019, that total was reduced to 3.7 million; and the company projected [before the impact of Covid] that the tally would be only 2 million in 2020, representing a 90.48% decline in printed textbook sales between 2010 and 2020. This metamorphosis, which the company projected would grow sharply in the years after 2021, meant that the company's allocations for printing (and paper and binding), warehousing, transporting, inventorying, and crediting returned or damaged printed books from college bookstores or distributors would decline at a rapid pace, impacting directly Pearson's bottom line. These facts appealed to Pearson's investors as well as the financial service analysts that covered Pearson's finances.[30]

The Movement Toward Digital Textbooks

Depressed sales triggered publisher's reviews of new and revised printed textbook title output. Again, looking at the printed chemistry book in Table 1.1, one strategy that gained traction after 2019 was to recognize, if not accept, substantive changes in the marketplace and the pernicious impact of the used and rental business. This meant that many textbook publishers, for example, reduced the number of printed copies of "big" college textbooks from 100,000 to about 50,000 units to reflect the harsh realities in the marketplace. Another major change included reducing the number of free printed copies provided to college faculty members (and relying on sending faculty members only digital copies of textbooks) since too many of these printed books, even those marked in bold letters on large adhesive labels on the front cover of books with "not for sale" or "instructor's copy" notations, ended up in the used or rental websites. The end results were significant financial reductions and larger profits.

These decisions triggered other changes. While the suggested retail price (SRP) for this representative printed chemistry text in 2000 was $110, in 2021 it was increased to $274.55 (+149.59%). Selling fewer domestic and foreign printed copies at a higher SRP generated a sharp increase in net revenues from $7,565,756 in 2000 to $9,007,193 in 2021 (+19.05%). While the cost of goods (COGS) was larger in 2021 ($5,535,547) versus $3,950,038 in 2000 (+40.14%), corporate contributions (e.g., the 20% overhead charge to cover various corporate functions including legal, information technology, rents, taxes, etc.) also increased from $1,513,151 in 2000 to $1,801,438 (+19.05%) in 2021. All of these changes did not help this book's bottom line; net profit declined from $1,038,567 in 2000 to only $297,208 in 2021 (−71.38%), and the important textbook's profit margin was a remarkably small +3.3% in 2021 versus a hefty +13.73% in 2000. Table 4.6 has the details.

Printed hardcover or paperback textbook unit manufacturing production costs increased sharply, prompting many of the "Big 5" firms to release both a printed and an e-textbook. The financial results of a digital book were impressive. Again, using the same printed chemistry textbook in Table 4.6, the digital version offered a number of cost savings. There were only digital e-textbook copies, thereby saving money since there were no allocations for printing, paper, binding, warehouse, distribution, and returns' expenses, and only digital copies were provided to faculty member to review for possible adoption. The SRP was $54.99 for the digital version for this chemistry e-text. There were costs, however, for plant, marketing, computer systems, and a small royalty advance against sales.

Total U.S. and export revenues for this digital e-textbook were $2,676,912 (U.S.: $1,724,486; exports $952,4260). Total cost of goods sold (COGS) reached $426,227, and corporate charges came in at $802,196. So, this meant that total sales reached $2,676,912 minus

Table 4.6 Sample P & L for a printed hardcover chemistry textbook (with a 3-year sales cycle) in 2021

Assumptions

---

736 page black & white and color text; four-color photographs, illustrations, and statistical tables; table of contents, glossary, and index; fine heavy paper; each copy weighs 3.6 pounds

Print run	50,000 copies
Free copies	1000 [author; editor; publishing house; sales representatives; faculty members for adoption review]
Gross sales	49,000 copies
Shipped	
U.S.	39,200 shipped copies
	7840 returned copies [U.S. 20.00% return rate; industry average for science textbooks in 2021]
	31,360 net
Exports	17,320
	0 returned copies [exports; sold as final sales]
	17,320 net
Never shipped/returned	320 copies
Suggested retail price (SRP)	$274.55 [Ege. *Organic Chemistry: Structure and Reactivity*]
Average discount	23% [U.S. $211.40 @ net to publisher]
	50% [exports $137.28 @ net to publisher]
PPB	$74.13 [27% of SRP; per unit × 50,000 copies]
Plant	$19.22 [7.0% of SRP; per unit × 50,000 copies]
Marketing	$27.46 [10.0% of SRP; per unit × 50,000 copies]
Royalty advance	$400,0000.00 [an advance against royalty rate of 10% domestic and 7% of exports; net price]
Other publishing income	$0
Total net revenues	
1. Sales: U.S.	$6,629,504.00 [39,200 − 7840 = 31,360 × $211.40]
2. Sales: exports	$2,377,689.00 [17,320 × $137.28]
3. Total sales	$9,007,193.00 [#8 + #9 = #10]
Cost of goods sold [COGS6]	
4. PPB	$3,706,500 [$74.13 per unit × 50,000 copies]
5. Plant	$961,000 [$19.22 per unit × 50,000 copies]
6. Earned royalty	$829,388.00 [total]
	[$662,950.00; 10% U.S. sales + $166,438.00; 7% of export sales]
7. Royalty write-off	$0.00 [Difference between advance and earned royalty]

(*continued*)

Table 4.6   (continued)

Assumptions	
8. Inventory write-off	$38,659.00 [320 copies remained in warehouse; PPB $74.13 + $19.22 Plant + $27.46 marketing = $120.81 × 320]
9. Total COGS	$5,535,547.00 [#11 + #12 + #13 +#14 + #15 = #16]
Corporate charges	
10. Marketing	$1,373,000.00 [$27.46 per unit × 50,000 copies]
11. Overhead 20% of total sales	$1,801,438.00 [20% of sales]
12. Total corporate charges	$3,174,438.00 [#17 + #18 = #19]
13. Total sales	$9,007,193.00 [#10]
14. Minus COGS	–$5,535,547.00[#16]
15. Minus corporate charges	–$3,174,438.00 [#19]
16. Net profit	$297,208.00 [#20 – #21 – #22 = #23]
17. Profit margin	3.30%

N.B. All numbers were rounded off and may not always equal 100%

COGS of $426,227 and minus corporate charges of $802,196, and the book generated a profit of $1,448,489 and an impressive profit margin of +54.11%. Table 4.7 has the details.

In 2000, the chemistry textbook in Table 1.1 posted a profit of $1,038,567 and a profit margin of +13.73%. The 2021 P & L for the printed chemistry book in Table 4.5 revealed a rather modest 3.30% profit margin and a net profit of only $297,208. Clearly, a digital textbook in 2021 required smaller financial allocations and human resources by the publisher, and the reduced financial allocations for an e-textbook generated a significantly higher profit. The data supported the argument that the publishers needed to abandon print for a digital marketplace. However, it is interesting that criticism emerged before and during the metamorphosis from in-person classroom instruction to computer screen teaching in March 2020 (the ubiquitous Zoom classes) that reading on a screen just might not be the best way for some students to learn.

So, the movement away from printed textbooks toward digital e-texts represented a fundamental and positive shift in the basic business marketing model for the "Big 5." However, there were marketing and technological issues that the publishers confronted. If a publisher released only new texts, or new editions of a text, as a digital textbook, would faculty members, possibly facing concerns from students about reading a text only on a computer screen, adopt a printed text from another publisher?

Table 4.7   Sample P & L for a digital chemistry textbook 2021: updated annually

Assumptions	
736 page black & white and color text (updated annually); four-color photographs; illustrations (changed annually); statistical tables (changed annually); table of contents, glossary, and index (changed annually); problems (changed annually); digital only version	
Print run	0 copies
Digital free copies	1000 [author, editor, publishing house, sales representatives, faculty members for adoption review]
Gross sales	48,600 copies
Shipped	
U.S.	31,360 sold digital copies
	0 returned copies
Exports	17,320
	0 returned copies
Never shipped/returned	0 copies
Suggested retail price (SRP)	$54.99 [Robinson, McMurry & Fay; *Chemistry, 8th edition* (Pearson)]
Average discount	0% [U.S. sales]
	0%
PPB	$0
Plant	$3.85 [7.0% of SRP; per unit × 48,600 copies]
Marketing	$5.49 [10.0% of SRP; per unit × 48,600 copies]
Royalty advance	$200,0000.00 [an advance against royalty rate of 10% domestic and 7% of export sales; net price]
Other publishing income	$0
Total net revenues	
1. Sales: U.S.	$1,724,486.00 [31,360 × $54.99] [#1]
2. Sales: exports	$952,426.00 [17,320 × $54.99] [#2]
3. Total sales	$2,676,912.00 [#1 + #2 = #3]
Cost of goods sold [COGS]	
4. PPB	$0
5. Plant	$187,110.00 [$3.85 per unit × 48,600 copies]

(*continued*)

Table 4.7   (continued)

Assumptions	
6. Earned royalty	$239,117.00 [total]
	[$172,448.00; 10% U.S. sales + $66,669.00; 7% of export sales]
7. Royalty write-off	$0 [Difference between advance and earned royalty]
8. Inventory write-off	$0
9. Total COGS	$426,227.00 [#4+ #5 + #6 +#7 + #8 = #9]
Corporate charges	
10. Marketing	$266,814.00 [$5.49 per unit × 48,600 copies]
11. Overhead 20% of total sales	$535,382.00 [20% of sales]
12. Total corporate charges	$802,196.00 [#10 + #11 = #12]
13. Total sales	$2,676,912.00 [#3]
14. Minus COGS	–$426,227.00 [#9]
15. Minus corporate charges[a]	–$802,196.00 [#12]
16. Net profit	$1,448,489.00 [#13 – #14 – #15 = #16]
17. Profit margin	54.11%

N.B. All numbers were rounded off and may not always equal 100%
[a]Will include any credit card swipe fees

How long would a student have access to the e-textbook? Some students need access to a text after the end of a course to prepare for board certification exams (e.g., accounting; nursing). Yet another concern centered on reading a digital text on a specific computer. Would a student be able to access a text on a tablet, laptop, and a desktop computer if the original laptop or computer were replaced with a newer unit? Of course, some faculty members were print oriented, and they might not be eager to read a digital textbook. While publishers could and did address these technological questions, they had to convince busy faculty members that unimpeded student access to a digital text would be guaranteed and that the portability of a digital textbook would make life easier for beleaguered faculty members and students.

While the textbook selling and publishing landscape appeared bleak, especially with the unsettling decision in the Kirtsaeng case, there were two positive legal development that would impact both college bookstores and text publishers.

THE REDIGI COPYRIGHT CASE: 2019

The first important case was the ReDigi case. It centered on the First Sale Doctrine, but the final legal outcome differed significantly from the Supreme Court's determination in the Kirtsaeng case. ReDigi, Inc. attempted to create a secondary resale market for digital products, specifically music. However, if ReDigi were able to launch a digital resale market, other digital products, including digital books, digital textbooks, and audiobooks could be sold by ReDigi. Capitol Records, LLC sued ReDigi in the Southern District of New York (SDNY) arguing that ReDigi's basic business model was a copyright infringement violation of the First Sale Doctrine in 17 U.S.C. §109(a).[31] ReDigi argued that their online digital resale market was permissible under the First Sale Doctrine of 17 U.S.C. §109(a) because of substantive technological changes.[32] The U.S. District Court entered a stipulated final judgment against ReDigi, awarding Capitol Records $3.5 million in damages and enjoining the operation of ReDigi.[33]

This case's determination triggered significant interest. Ben Sisario, in *The New York Times*, opined that this decision "dealt a blow to the nascent business of reselling digital goods like music and books."[34] Mary Minow, in *Library Journal*, also viewed this decision as a major defeat for reselling digital products. "Libraries and friends groups interested in reselling or giving away used e-books or other digital content files (or purchasing them), may be a little more cautious after the March 30 [ReDigi] decision."[35]

ReDigi appealed this decision to the Second Circuit arguing that the First Sale Doctrine should apply. The Association of American Publishers (AAP), aware of the potential negative impact a resale market posed for the then growing market of digital books and audiobooks, filed an *amicus curiae* brief with the Second Circuit. The AAP maintained that "the judgment of the District Court should be affirmed... The Court correctly rejected the two principal affirmative defenses proffered by ReDigi, i.e., the first sale defense under § 109(a) of the Copyright Act (hereafter the 'Act') and the fair use defense under § 107. As the District Court explained, the first-sale defense under § 109(a) does not apply to ReDigi's conduct for at least two reasons. First, § 109(a) by its terms only provides a defense to violations of the copyright owner's exclusive right of distribution under § 106(3); it offers no defense for infringements of Capitol's exclusive right of reproduction under § 106(1), which ReDigi violated by making unauthorized reproductions: SPA-11-13. Second, even with respect to ReDigi's unauthorized distribution of the recordings, ReDigi is not eligible for a first-sale defense under § 109(a) because the phonorecords it distributed were not the same tangible copies of which it was the lawful owner, as § 109(a) requires, but were instead newly-created tangible copies...."[36]

The AAP then focused explicitly on the e-book market. "The threat ReDigi itself poses to book publishers is not hypothetical. ReDigi has long expressed its intention to build its company around 'used' eBooks... Any ruling in ReDigi's favor on this appeal would therefore have immediate and profoundly damaging consequences for the publishing industry, even beyond the significant threat posed by ReDigi itself...."[37]

The Second Circuit supported the decision of the Southern District of New York and rejected ReDigi's First Sale defense.[38] ReDigi decided to submit a petition of a writ of *certiorari* to the Supreme Court of the United States citing the First Sale defense utilized by Kirtsaeng.[39] In this writ, ReDigi presented three questions for the Supreme Court: "1. Under 17 U.S.C. § 109(a), is the acknowledged owner of a particular digital phonorecord lawfully purchased via electronic distribution under 17 U.S.C. § 106(3) entitled to freely alienate that digital phonorecord electronically? 2. Consistent with the first sale and exhaustion doctrines embodied in 17 U.S.C. § 109(a), can the electronic disposition of a lawfully acquired digital phonorecord simultaneously violate the copyright owner's exclusive right of reproduction under 17 U.S.C. § 106(1) even though no additional copies or phonorecords are created? 3. If yes, is the alleged violation of the reproduction right nonetheless a fair use under 17 U.S. C. § 107?"[40]

The Supreme Court decided, on June 24, 2019, not to hear ReDigi's appeal, and they let the earlier decision stand.[41] So, under the terms of the First Sale Doctrine, it remains illegal to resell a digital product, including music, an e-book, an e-textbook, or an audiobook, in the U.S. It is also illegal in the European Union (EU) due to a ruling by the Court of Justice of the European Union (CJEU) in the "Tom Kabinet" case C-263/18 "that the sale of 'second-hand' e-books through a website constitutes communication to the public and therefore requires the consent of the rightholder..."[42]

Appeals to the Supreme Court can be a rather complex, long, and a very costly procedure, but it did seem odd that the Court used the First Sale Doctrine in Kirtsaeng but rejected to hear that argument in ReDigi even though many of the organizations that supported Kirtsaeng with *amicus curiae* briefs also supported ReDigi. Perhaps the Court viewed printed physical products in a different light than digital products, including e-books or audiobooks. Perhaps we will never know exactly why the Court declined to hear this appeal.

A Second Major Legal Victory for College Bookstores and Textbook Publishers

While the ReDigi case was a major victory for book publishers, the economic outlook for new printed textbooks remained somewhat "uncertain." Out of the blue emerged an obscure ruling from the U.S. Department of Education (Education) that offered beleaguered college bookstores and text publishers a "golden opportunity" to address directly the threats posed by the increasing successes of online sites selling used and renting printed textbooks.

On July 1, 2016, the U.S. Department of Education's "Rule 164" went into effect.[43] This rule stipulated that colleges "may include the costs of books and supplies as part of tuition and fees;" the books or supplies must be "below competitive market rates..."[44] And a student may opt out of the program. This procedure became known as Inclusive Access (IA).

Rule 164 included the following terms and conditions. "The amount incurred by the student for the payment period for purchasing books, supplies, and other educationally related goods and services provided by the institution [i.e. college or university] for which the institution obtains the student's or parent's authorization under... An institution may include the costs of books and supplies as part of tuition and fees... The institution—(a) Has an arrangement with a book publisher or other entity that enables it to make those books or supplies available to students below competitive market rates; (b) Provides a way for a student to obtain those books and supplies by the seventh day of a payment period; and (c) Has a policy under which the student may opt out of the way the institution provides for the student to obtain books and supplies under this paragraph (c)(2)... The institution documents on a current basis that the books or supplies, including digital or electronic course materials, are not available elsewhere or accessible by students enrolled in that program from sources other than those provided or authorized by the institution..."[45]

While many individuals viewed Education's Rule 164 as a college text-book provision, in reality the language of the rule referred specifically to "books or supplies available to students." This phrase was used because other types of books were also required frequently by college professors, which included a rather wide variety of "books" (i.e., trade books, scholarly books published by university presses and commercial scholarly publishers, and professional books released by commercial publishers).

It was clear to the college bookstore sector and textbook publishers that Rule 164 was a mechanism for those entities to reclaim part of the business they lost to various online sites offering used and rental books, a fact that also captured the attention of important financial service companies that held stock in many of the "Big 5" publishers. However, to utilize the rule, colleges had to agree to accept and follow the terms and conditions of the rule, and this meant approaching and signing colleges to adopt IA (sometimes called "First Day"), and this process was time consuming. Another problem centered on the fact that each publisher offered different IA terms and conditions with different discount cost structures for various academic fields. According to Pearson, most Inclusive Access prices "averaged" about 50–70% lower than the cost of the printed text,[46] an estimate that appeared to be followed by Wiley[47] and Macmillan Learning.[48] The Association of American Publishers (AAP), the nation's largest and most important publishing trade association, supported the IA option, especially since a student could opt out of participating in an IA option. AAP, concerned about the digital disruption that undermined textbook publishers, stressed the need for IA in this nation, and they issued a comprehensive document that emphasized the pressing need for IA. "Inclusive Access is a course material delivery model that helps institutions of higher education provide students with access to course materials on the first day of class, at a discounted price. Inclusive Access offers the following benefits: accessible, interactive, and personalized digital content; first-day access to digital course materials, which has proven to increase student retention and performance in class." AAP also mentioned that Title IV of the Higher Education Act stipulated that "if Title IV monies are used for Inclusive Access, then the educational materials provided are required by Federal regulations to be priced below competitive market rates—so students get a discount..."[49]

IA: NEGATIVE RESPONSES AND ANTITRUST LITIGATION

Not all of the responses to IA were positive. Over the years, the U.S. Public Interest Research Group (PIRG) has been very active in analyzing college textbook costs. In a detailed report about IA, PIRG maintained that IA prevented students from shopping around to get the best price for a new, used, or rented textbook, effectively handcuffing students to an anticompetitive system that benefited only bookstores and publishers.[50] A number of reporters writing for different publications supported PIRG's concerns.[51]

The intrinsic concern, and in some instances antagonism, toward IA triggered a series of nine antitrust law suits with very different plaintiffs (e.g., ironically off-campus bookstores were plaintiffs) and defendants (e.g., Barnes & Noble, Follett, college textbook publishers) in various jurisdictions (e.g., South Carolina, Delaware, Illinois, New Jersey).[52] The Educational Publishers Enforcement Group (EPEG) was also listed in several law suits. EPEG members included Elsevier, Cengage, Macmillan Learning, McGraw-Hill, and Pearson.[53]

However, the legal thread underlining all of the litigation centered clearly on the allegation that the various defendants had participated in an illegal conspiracy to create a system that was, in essence, a restraint of free trade and, therefore, a violation of the Sherman Act of 1890 and the Clayton Act of 1914. Apparently, the various lawyers for the plaintiffs decided it was easier to initiate litigation against college textbook publishers, and their trade association, rather than go after the publishers of trade, scholarly, and professional books since almost all of the public criticisms about IA addressed the pricing strategies of traditional textbooks.

The relevant section of The Sherman Act of 1890 (15 U.S.C.) §1 included, "Every contract, combination in the form of trust or otherwise, or conspiracy, in restraint of trade or commerce among the several States, or with foreign nations, is declared to be illegal. Every person who shall make any contract or engage in any combination or conspiracy hereby declared to be illegal shall be deemed guilty of a felony..."[54]

The Clayton Act of 1914 (15 U.S.C.) §15 stated that "except as provided in subsection (b), any person who shall be injured in his business or property by reason of anything forbidden in the antitrust laws may sue therefor in any district court of the United States in the district in which the defendant resides or is found or has an agent, without respect to the amount in controversy, and shall recover threefold the damages by him sustained, and the cost of suit, including a reasonable attorney's fee..."[55]

Some of the defendants (e.g., McGraw-Hill, Pearson, Cengage, Barnes & Noble, Follett) petitioned, under 28 U.S.C. §1407, to the United States Judicial Panel on Multidistrict Litigation (MDL) that the nine law suits be consolidated into one antitrust law suit in Delaware. The appeal was granted on August 11, 2020, by the Judicial Panel on Multidistrict Litigation, and the lawsuits were consolidated into "In Re Inclusive Access Course Materials Antitrust Litig.; 20 MDL No. 2946, DCL; United States District Court Southern District of New York" (and not Delaware). Judge Denise L. Cote presided over the case, and a jury trial was waived in the consolidated document.[56]

The introductory section in the consolidated law suit[57] listed the following substantive material. "The Representative Student Purchaser Plaintiffs (Plaintiffs), by and through their attorneys, bring this action (Action) on behalf of themselves and all others situated against the three dominant publishers of college and graduate school textbooks, Cengage Learning Inc. (Cengage), McGraw Hill LLC (McGraw Hill), and Pearson Education, Inc. (Pearson; collectively, the Publisher Defendants), and against the two dominant operators of official on-campus college and university bookstores, Barnes & Noble College Booksellers, LLC and Barnes & Noble Education, Inc. (collectively Barnes & Noble; B&N), and Follett Education Group, Inc. (Follett; and collectively with B&N, the Reseller Defendants; and collectively the Publisher Defendants and the Reseller Defendants are referred to as the defendants)."[58]

The plaintiffs maintained strenuously that the defendants participated in the IA program in what they maintained were "unlawful agreements" and that the defendants created a system "to artificially reduce the supply of printed textbooks for the purpose of limiting the volume of sales that feed the secondary market…"[59] In addition, they insisted that "cooperation among the Publisher Defendants was critical to the expansion of Inclusive Access…" Since the publishers "control nearly 90% of the university textbook marketplace…" in what the plaintiffs alleged was an "oligopolistic structure of the publishing industry [due to] the product of several mergers…"[60] The plaintiffs also alleged that "the defendants have opportunities to collude at meetings of the trade association EPEG and NACS…" in what the plaintiffs argued was "a series of agreements in restraint of trade…"[61] To support their allegations that the "defendant's anticompetitive scheme harms students," the plaintiffs submitted a series of detailed document to the presiding Judge.[62] The plaintiffs also alleged that "the Student Purchaser Plaintiffs have suffered antitrust injury as a result of the Defendants' conduct… [and] the defendants concealed their Scheme from the representative Student Purchaser Plaintiffs and other members of the class…"[63]

Specifically, the plaintiffs alleged that they had legal standing to initiate this litigation, were impacted negatively by the defendant's violation of relevant sections of both Sherman and Clayton, and sustained financial losses because they were unable to "shop around" to find the best prices for textbooks. They listed six claims for relief.[64]

Judge Cote reviewed the relevant provision of Sherman and Clayton, the history of Rule 164, the history of the litigation in the nine law suits, the consolidated ruling, the extensive legal documents submitted by attorneys for the plaintiffs and the defendants, and the motion by the defendants to dismiss the case because the plaintiffs lacked legal standing under Rule 12(b), Federal Rules of Civil Procedures.[65] Judge Cote addressed specifically the plaintiff's allegations.[66] In her detailed ruling, Judge Cote ruled that all of the plaintiff's six claims were flawed.[67] The Judge's "Conclusion" stated that "the Defendant's January 22, 2021, motion to dismiss was granted. The Clerk of the Court shall close the case and enter judgement for the Defendants."[68] On June 15, 2021, the Clerk issued the "Ordered, Adjudged, and Decreed" document that stated that "for the reasons stated in the Court's Opinion and Order dated June 14, 2021, the Defendants' January 22, 2021, motions to dismiss are granted, judgment is entered for the defendants, and the case is closed."[69]

Conclusion

The entire textbook industry, bookstores and publishers, achieved two significant legal victories in both the ReDigi and IA[70] cases, and they withstood the impact of the Covid lockdowns. However, their search for clarity, certainty, competitive advantage, and scale between 2019 and 2021 proved to be, at best, somewhat successful and, at worst, a harbinger of future set-backs and disappointments.

Notes

1. Congress.gov. "H.R. 2107," www.congress.gov/bill/116th-congress/house-bill/2107/text. Also see Scholarly Publishing and Academic Resource Center (SPARC). "The Affordable College Textbook Act,"

https://sparcopen.org/our-work/affordable-college-textbook-act. SPARC, "Make college textbooks more affordable," https://sparcopen. org/wp=content/uploads/2019/04/Fact_Sheet_Affordable_College_ Textbook_Act.pdf.

2. J. Falk. "OpenStax To Vastly Expand Open Education Library with Support from National Foundations," https://openstax.org/press/ openstax-vastly-expand-open-education-library-support-national-foundations. Also see C. Reid. "2.2M Students Used OpenStax Free Textbooks in 2018," www.publishersweekly.com/pw/by-topic/digital/ content-and-e-books/article/79320-2-2m-students-used-openstax-free-textbooks-in-2018.html. OpenStax. "Who We Are," https://openstax. org; OpenStax. Research mission (2020), https://openstax.org/research. J. Pate. "Supporting Students: OER and Textbook Affordability Initiatives at a Mid-Sized University," ir.una.edu/libfacpresentation/45. E. Rhodes. "Opening the book on Open Educational Resources," www.libraryjournal.com/?detailStory=Opening-the-book-on-Open-Educational-Resources. N.L. Maron. "Opening the Textbook: New Opportunities for Libraries and Publishers," sr.ithaka.org/wp=content/uploads/2014/03/ SR_BriefingPaper_Textbook_20140306.pdf. L. McKenna. "Why Students Are Still Spending So Much for College Textbooks," *The Atlantic*, www. theatlantic.com/education/archive/2018/01/why-students-are-still-spending-so-much-for-college-textbooks/551639.

3. Business Wire. "Barnes & Noble Education Retains Financial Advisor to Assist in Previously Announced Strategic Review," www.businesswire. com/news/home/20200108005098/en/Barnes-Noble-Education-Retains-Financial-Advisor-to-Assist-in-Previously-Announced-Strategic-Review. Business Wire. "Barnes & Noble Education Reports Third Quarter Fiscal Year 2020 Financial Results," www.businesswire.com/news/ home/20200303005233/en/Barnes-Noble-Education-Reports-Third-Quarter-Fiscal-Year-2020-Financial-Results. Seeking Alpha. "Barnes & Noble Education Furloughs Employees," https://seekingalpha.com/ news/3558034-barnes-noble-education-furloughs-employees.

4. Business Wire. "Barnes & Noble Education Reports Fourth Quarter and Fiscal Year 2020 Financial Results," www.businesswire.com/news/ home/20200714005249/en/Barnes-Noble-Education-Reports-Fourth-Quarter-and-Fiscal-Year-2020-Financial-Results#:~:text=Financial%20 results%20for%20the%20fourth,compared%20to%20the%20prior%20year. Barnes & Noble Education. "News Release Details," https://investor. bned.com/investor-relations/news-abd-events/news/press-release-details/2020/Barnes-Noble-Education-reports-first   quarter-fiscal-year-2021-financial-results/default.aspx. Barnes & Noble Education.

"Annual Report [May 1, 2021)," https://d18rn0p25nwr6d.cloudfront. net/CIK-0001634117/7384acfd-8477-4f3d-b5a7-90130409ece7.pdf.

5. Milliot. "B &NE Retail Segment Took Big Hit in Q1," www.publisher-sweekly.com/pw/by-topic/industry-news/bookselling/article/84255-b-ne-retail-segment-took-big-hit-in-q1.html. Seeking Alpha. "Barnes & Noble Education: Growing Digital Solutions Helping to Turn the Page," https://seekingalpha.com/article/4394411-barnes-noble-education-growing-digital-solutions-helping-to-turn-page. M. Maurer. "Barnes & Noble Education CFO Eyes More Cuts as Campuses Remain Closed," www.wsj.com/articles/barnes-noble-education-cfo-eyes-more-cuts-as-campuses-remain-closed-11609165800. J. Rosen. "College Stores Adapt to Change," https://www.publishersweekly.com/pw/by-topic/industry-news/bookselling/article/79300-college-stores-adapt-to-change.html

6. B. Chappatta. "Back-to-School Doubts Crush Textbook Publishers," www.bloomberg.com/opinion/articles/2020-08-20/covid-19-back-to-school-doubts-crush-textbook-publishers.

7. Pearson. "Interim Results for the Six Months to 30th June 2020 (Unaudited)," www.pearson.com/content/dam/one-dot-com/one-dot-com/global/Files/news/news-annoucements/2020/Pearson-2020-Interim-Results-Press-Release-24-July-2020.pdf?source=news_body_link. Also see Seeking Alpha. "Pearson: Digital Disruption Is a Double-Edged Sword," https://seekingalpha.com/article/4391644-pearson-digital-disruption-is-double-edged-sword. A. Barker. "Pearson Chief John Fallon to Retire Next Year," www.ft.com/content/61ad7db4-2166-11ea-b8a1-584213ee7b2b. C. Ryan. "A Learning Curve for Pearson's New Boss," www.wsj.com/articles/a-learning-curve-for-pearsons-new-boss-11600444917.

8. Seeking Alpha. "Cengage Learning Holdings II, Inc. (CNGO) CEO Michael Hansen on Q3 2020 results—Earnings call Transcript," https://seekingalpha.com/symbol/CNGO/earnings/transcripts. Also see Cengage Learning. "Q4 and Fiscal Year 2020: Investor Update," https://cengage.widen.net/content/rdxihgdqzp/pdf/Q4-FY20-Investor-Financials-V-FINAL-20200617-1900.pdf?u=fn2gt2. Cengage Learning. "Second Quarter Fiscal 2021: Investor Update," https://cengage.widen.net/content/uq9wpv1xtn/pdf/Q2-FY21-Investor-Financials-FINAL-11.11-vFFF.pdf?u=fn2gt2.

9. McGraw-Hill Education, Inc. "McGraw-Hill Fiscal 2021 Q1 Investor Update," https://s22.q4cdn.com/942918855/files/doc_financials/2021/q1/MH-FY-Q1-2021-Investor-Update-Final-8.28.20.pdf. McGraw-Hill Education, Inc. "McGraw-Hill Fiscal 2021 Q2 Investor Update," https://investors.mheducation.com/financial-information/quarterly-results/default.aspx. Fitch Ratings. "Fitch Affirms McGraw-Hill's IDR at B+; Outlook Revised to Negative," www.fitchratings.com/

research/corporate-finance/fitch-affirms-houghton-mifflin-idr-at-b-outlook-revised-to-negative-18-05-2020. Fitch Rating., "Fitch Affirms MHGE's IDR at B+; Rates 1.5 Lien Debt BB; Downgrades SR Unsecured to BB-," www.fitchratings.com/research/corporate-finance/fitch-affirm-mhge-idr-at-b-rates-1-5-lien-debt-bb-downgrades-sr-unsecured-to-bb-15-12-2020. Yahoo Finance. "McGraw-Hill Education, Inc. McGraw Hill Launches Transaction to Refinance Its Near-Term Debt," https://finance.yahoo.com/news/mcgraw-hill-launches-transaction-refinance-222800660.html. A "BB" rating indicates a high probability of default; a "BB-" rating indicates a higher level of concern that deteriorating economic conditions and/or company-specific developments could hinder the issuer's ability to meet its obligations.

10. The Mottley Fool. "John Wiley & Sons., Inc. (JW-A) (JW-B) Q3 2020 Earnings Call Transcript," www.fool.com/earnings/call-transcripts/2020/03/04/john-wiley-sons-inc-jw-a-jw-b-q3-2020-earnings-cal.aspx. The Mottley Fool. "John Wiley & Sons., Inc. (JW-A) (JW-B) Q4 2020 Earnings Call Transcript," www.fool.com/earnings/call-transcripts/2020/06/12/john-wiley-sons-inc-jwa-jwb-q4-2020-earnings-call.aspx. Seeking Alpha. "John Wiley & Sons Should See Benefit From Virtual Shift," https://seekingalpha.com/article/4388363-john-wiley-sons-should-see-benefit-from-virtual-shift. J. Milliot. "Wiley Has Sharp Earnings in Q2," www.publishersweekly.com/pw/by-topic/industry-news/financial-reporting/article/85084-wiley-has-sharp-earnings-increase-in-q2.html.

11. National Association of College Stores (NACS). "NACS Report: Student Spending on Course Materials Continues to Decline," https://www.nacs.org/student-spending-on-course-materials-continues-to-decline. Also see NACS. "Industry," https://www.oncampusresearch.org/faculty-watch. NACS. "Student Watch," https://www.oncampusresearch.org/student-watch.

12. B. Gates. "What I Learned from Warren Buffett," https://hbr.org/1996/01/what-i-learned-from-warren-buffett. Also see E. Manditch. "Can Economic Moats Provide Investors with a Competitive Advantage?" www.creativematter.skidmore.edu/econ_studt_schol/95. D.P. Boyd. "Financial Metrics in Wide-Moat Firms," *Journal of Business and Economics Research*, 4, 6(June 2006), 59–63.

13. M.E. Porter. "The Five Competitive Forces that Shape Strategy," *Harvard Business Review*, 86, 1(January 2008), 78–93.

14. W. Chan Kim, R. Mauborgne. *Blue Ocean Strategy: How to Create Uncontested Market Space and Make the Competition Irrelevant* (Boston: Harvard Business Review Press, 2015), pp. 3–24, 103–116.

15. I worked in labor relations (e.g., collective bargaining; grievances and arbitrations; an advisor to Taft-Hartley Trust Funds; etc.) in the commercial printing industry in New York, New Jersey, and Connecticut, and I had an office in a New York City brownstone building on East 73rd Street between 5th Avenue and Madison Avenue. The actor Roy Scheider lived a few doors away, and we went for breakfast to the same coffee shop. Roy was a very friendly individual, and he talked with patrons about his acting career. One day he mentioned that this famous line in *Jaws*, often considered one of the most famous lines in Hollywood's history, was an "ad lib;" it was not in the script. He just saw the shark for the first time, walked into the cabin, and told Quint "You're gonna need a bigger boat." This quote has become part of the business school vocabulary.

16. The Federal Trade Commission. "The Antitrust Laws," www.ftc.gov/tips-advice/competition-guidance/guide-antitrust-laws/antitrust-laws.

17. McGraw Hill. "Cengage and McGraw Hill to Merge, Providing Students with More Affordable Access to Superior Course Materials and Platforms," www.mheducation.com/news-media/press-releases/cengage-mcgraw-hill-merge.html.

18. M. Bartz. "U.S. College Education Could be Pricier with Textbook Merger," www.reuters.com/article/us-cengage-m-a-mcgrawhill/-u-s-college-education-could-be-pricer-with-textbook-merger-idUSKCN1UO135?il-0. Also see G. Blumenstyk. "Planned Merger of Cengage and McGraw Hill Could Remake College-Textbook Market," www.chronicle.com/article/Planned-Merger-of-Cengage-and/246224. Bartz. "College Textbook Merger Raises 'Serious Concern' Among U.S. Lawmakers," www.nytimes.com/reuters/2020/03/10/business/10reuters-megrawhill-m-a-cengage.html. A. Swaminathan. "The Textbook Market Is Broken, and the Largest Mega-Merger Makes It Worse," https://finance.yahoo.com/news/textbooks-college-deal-165350614.html. S. Gillen. "Textbook Publisher Mergers and Acquisitions: What Authors Need to Know," https://blog.taaonline.net/2019/07/textbook-publisher-mergers-and-acquisitions-what-authoprs-need-to-know. J. Berman. "What the McGraw-Hill, Cengage Merger Means for Textbook Prices," www.marketwatch.com/story/mcgraw-hill-and-cengage-are-merging-what-that-means-for-college-textbook-prices-2019-05-02. N. Allen. "Q & A: Cengage/McGraw-Hill Merger," https://sparcopen.org/news/2019/qa-cengage-mcgraw-hill-merger.

19. J. Lewin. "Textbook Publisher to Rent to College Students," www.nytimes.com/2009/08/14/education/14textbook.html.

20. *Ibid.*

21. *Ibid.*

22. United States Courts. "Chapter 11: Bankruptcy Basics," www.uscourts. gov/services-forms/bankruptcy/bankruptcy-basics/chapter-11-bankruptcy-basics. Also see Anon. "Dealbook. Cengage Learning Files for Bankruptcy,"   www.dealbook.nytimes.com/2013/07/02/ cengage-learning-files-for-bankruptcy.

23. J.A. Trachtenberg. "McGraw-Hill Sells Education to Apollo," www.wsj. com/articles/SB10001424127887323330604578143001164607408. Also see Apollo Global Management, Inc. "About Apollo," www.apollo. com/about-apollo.

24. Apollo Global Management, Inc. Apollo is a high growth alternative asset manager; https://www.apollo.com.

25. Pearson. "Print Rental Program," www.pearson.com/us/higher-education/customers/college-resellers/print-rental-program.html. Also see R. Kelly. "Pearson Expands Textbook Rental Program," www.campustechnology.com/articles/2017/04/21/pearson-expands-textbook-rental-program.aspx.

26. Pearson. "Pearson 2017 Preliminary Results [Unaudited]," www.pearson. com/content/dam/one-dot-com/one-dot=com/global/Files/news/ news-announcements/2018/Pearson=2017-Full-Year-Results\Press-Release-February=2018-2.pdf. Pearson. "Pearson 2018 Preliminary Results [Unaudited]," www.pearson.com/content/dam/one-dot-com/ one-dot=com/global/Files/news/news-announcements/2019/2018-Prelim-Results-Press-Release-financials-20190222.pdf. Pearson. "Pearson 2019 Preliminary Results [Unaudited]," www.pearson.com/content/ dam/one-dot-com/one-dot=com/global/Files/news/news-announcements/2020/2019-full-year=and-financials.pdf.   Pearson. "Pearson Annual Report and Accounts 2019," www.pearson.com/content/dam/one-dot-com/one=dot-com/global/standalone/ ar2019/2019-ar.pdf. Pearson. "2020 Interim Results," www.pearson. com/content/dam/one-dot-com/one-dot-com/global/Files/news/ news-annoucements/2020/Interims-2020-Presentation_Web.pdf.

27. Pearson. "Pearson 2020 Q1 Trading Update [Unaudited]," www.pearson.com/news-and-research/announcements/2020/04/pearson-2020-q1-trading-update%2D%2Dunaudited-.html. Also see Pearson. "January Trading Update," www.pearson.com/content/dam/one-dot-com/one-dot-com/global/Files/news/news-annoucements/2020/Pearson-2020-January-Trading-Update-Presentation_Web.pdf.   Pearson. "Interim Results for the Six Months to June 30th, 2020," www.pearson.com/ content/dam/one-dot-com/one-dot-com/global/Files/news/news-annoucements/2020/Pearson-2020-Interim-Results-Press-Release-24-July-2020.pdf. McKinsey & Company. "The Future of Textbooks,"

www.mckinsey.com/industries/public-and-social-sector/our-insights/
the-future-of-textbooks.

28. J. Milliot. "Pearson Strikes Textbook Rental Deal with NACS," www.pub-
    lishersweekly.com/pw/by-topic/industry-news/bookselling/
    article/73388-pearson-strikes-textbook-rental-deal-with-nacs.html. Also
    see C. Peukert. "The Next Wave of Digital Technological Change and the
    Cultural Industries." *Journal of Cultural Economics*, 43, 2 (2019), 189–210.
29. Seeking Alpha. "Pearson Rebounds as Credit Suisse Sees 'Damage' Done,"
    https://seekingalpha.com/news/3544923-pearson-rebounds-credit-
    suisse-sees-damage-done.
30. Pearson. "Pearson Creates New Direct-to-Consumer Division," www.
    pearson.com/news-and-research/announcements/2020/11/pearson-
    creates-new-direct-to-consumer-division.
    html#:~:text=LONDON%2C%2018th%20NOVEMBER%2C%20
    2020%3A,with%20learners%20around%20the%20world. Also see Pearson.
    "Pearson Annual Report and Accounts 2019," www.pearson.com/con-
    tent/dam/one-dot-com/one-dot-com/global/standalone/
    ar2019/2019-ar.pdf. Pearson. "2020 Interim Results," www.pearson.
    com/content/dam/one-dot-com/one-dot-com/global/Files/news/
    news-annoucements/2020/Interims-2020-Presentation_Web.pdf.
    Pearson. "Pearson PLC (PSO) Q3 2020 Earnings Call Transcript," www.
    fool.com/earnings/call-transcripts/2020/10/14/pearson-plc-pso-
    q3-2020-earnings-call-transcript. Ernst & Young (E & Y). "How to
    Accelerate Online Direct to Consumer Strategies beyond Covid-19,"
    www.ey.com/en_us/consumer-products-retail/how-to-accelerate-online-
    direct-to-consumer-strategies-beyond-covid-19. L. Schlesinger.
    "Reinventing the Direct-to-Consumer Business Model," https://hbr.
    org/2020/03/reinventing-the-direct-to-consumer-business-model.
31. United States District Court Southern District of New York(SDNY).
    "Capitol Records, LLC, Plaintiff, v. ReDigi INC., Defendant. 934 F.
    Supp.2d 640 (2013)," www.copyright.gov/fair-use/summaries/capitol-
    records-llc-redigi-inc-no.16-2321-2nd-cir.dec.12.2018.pdf.
32. *Ibid.*
33. *Ibid.*
34. B. Sisario. "A Setback For Resellers of Digital Products," www.nytimes.
    com/2013/04/02/business/media/redigi-loses-suit-over-reselling-of-
    digital-music.html.
35. M. Minow. "Selling Used Digital Files: A Setback, But Not the End of the
    Story," www.libraryjournal.com/?detailStory=selling-used-digital-files-a-
    setback-but-not-the-end-of-the-story. Also see J.D. Shulman,
    A.T. Coughlan. "Used Goods, Not Used Bads: Profitable Secondary

Market Sales for a Durable Goods Channel," *Quantitative Marketing and Economics*, 5, 2(June 2007), 191–210.

36. United States Court of Appeals for the Second Circuit. "16-2321-cv. Capitol Records, LLC, Capitol Christian Music Group, Inc., Virgin Records IR Holdings, Inc. Plaintiffs-Appellees v. ReDigi Inc., John Ossenmacher, Larry Rudolf, aba Lawrence Rogel, Defendants-Appellants. On Appeal from the United States District Court for the Southern District of New York. Brief of Amicus Curiae Association of American Publishers, Inc. in Support of Plaintiffs-Appellees," https://publishers.org/wp-content/uploads/2019/12/briefofamicuscuriaeassociationofamerican-publishers.pdf?10000.

37. *Ibid.*

38. United States Court of Appeals for the Second Circuit. 16-2321-cv. https://law.justia.com/cases/federal/appellate-courts/ca2/16-2321/16-2321-2018-12-12.html.

39. In The Supreme Court of the United States. "ReDigi Inc., John Ossenmacher, Larry -Rudolf, aba Lawrence Rogel, Petitioners v. Capitol Records, LLC, Capitol Christian Music Group, Inc., Virgin Records IR Holdings, Inc., Respondents. On Petition for a Writ of Certiorari to the United States Court of Appeal for the Second Circuit," www.supreme-court.gov/DocketPDF/18/18-1430/99242/20190510113929702_ReDigi%20Inc%20v%20Capitol%20Records%20Petition%20for%20a%20Writ%20of%20Certiorari.pdf.

40. *Ibid.*

41. K. Jahner. "Justices Let Stand Record Companies' Win Over Digital Resales," https://news.bloomberglaw.com/ip-law/justices-let-stand-record-companies-win-over-digital-resales.

42. A. Kaiser. "Exhaustion, Distribution, and Communication to the Public—The CJEU's Decision C-263/18—Tom Kabinet on e-Books and Beyond," *GRUR International*, 69, 5 (May 2020), 489-495. Also see Anon. "Tom Kabinet," *IIC—International review of Intellectual Property and Competition Law*, 51, 6 (May 2020), 772. D. Meyer. "Why the Second-Hand e-Book Market May Never Take Off," www.fortune.com/2019/12/19/used-ebooks-resell-market-eu-court.

43. Office of the Federal Register, National Archives and Records Administration. "*34 CFR § 668.164 - Disbursing funds...* [Government]. Office of the Federal Register, National Archives and Records Administration," https://www.govinfo.gov/app/details/CFR-2016-title34-vol3/CFR-2016-title34-vol3-sec668-164.

44. *Ibid.*

45. *Ibid.*

46. Pearson. "Terms of [Inclusive Access] Use," www.pearson.com/en-us/legal-information/terms-of-use.html. Pearson. "8 Myths About Inclusive Access," www.pearson.com/us/campaigns/faculty-inclusive-access-myths.html.
47. John Wiley. "Wiley Inclusive Access," www.wiley.com/learn/inclusive-access.
48. Macmillan Learning. "Macmillan Learning Inclusive Access," www.macmillanlearning.com/college/us/solutions/inclusive-access.
49. AAP. "College Course Materials Q & A: Frequently Asked Questions About Student Spending on Course Materials and Inclusive Access Programs," www.publishers.org/wp-content/uploads/2020/05/Inclusive-Access-FAQ1.pdf. Also see Congress.gov. "H.R. 2107," www.congress.gov/bill/116th-congress/house-bill/2107/text.
50. U.S. PIRG. "Automatic Textbook Billing: An Offer Students Can't Refuse"; https://uspirg.org/sites/pirg/files/reports/Automatic-Textbook-Billing/USPIRG_Textbook-Automatic-Billing_Feb2020.pdf. Also see U.S. PIRG. "Fixing the Broken Textbook Market, Third Edition," https://pirg.org/edfund/resources/fixing-the-broken-textbookmarket-third-edition.
51. R. Koenig. "When Colleges Sign 'Inclusive Access' Textbook Deals, Can Students and Professors Opt Out?" https://www.edsurge.com/news/2020-02-27-when-colleges-sign-inclusive-access-textbook-deals-can-students-and-professors-opt-out. J.R. Young. "Colleges Are Striking Bulk Deals with Textbook Publishers. Critics Say There Are Many Downsides," https://www.edsurge.com/news/2019-05-23-colleges-are-striking-bulk-deals-with-textbook-publishers-critics-say-there-are-many-downsides. T. Swaak. "Do 'Inclusive Access' Textbook Programs Save Students Money? A New Site Urges Everyone to Read the Fine Print," https://www.chronicle.com/article/do-inclusive-access-textbook-programs-save-students-money-a-new-site-urges-everyone-to-read-the-fine-print.html. A. Carrns. "That Digital Textbook? Your College Has Billed You For It," https://www.nytimes.com/2020/20/28/your-money/college-digital-textbooks.html. J.J.Jenkins, L.A. Sanchez, M.A.K. Schraedley, J. Hannans, J. Navick, J. Young. "Textbook Broke: Textbook Affordability As A Social Justice Issue," https://jime.open.ac.uk/article/10.5334/jime.549. E. Shaak. "Class Action Says Textbook Publishers' Inclusive Access Product Harms Independent Booksellers, Raises Prices for Students," https://www.classaction.org/blog/class-action-says-textbooks-publishers-inclusive-access-product-harms-independent-booksellers-raises-prices-for-students.
52. The list of law suits include the following. Virginia Pirate Corporation v. Trident Technical College Enterprise Campus Authority, Mary Thornsley;

United States District Court for the District of South Carolina Charleston Division; Civil Action No. 2:19-cv-00276-DCN. Also see Campus Book Company, Inc.; BJJ Corporation; CBSKY, Inc.; CBSNM, Inc.; and Renttext.com, Inc. v. McGraw Global Education Holdings, LLC; Pearson Education, Inc.; Cengage Learning, Inc.; Barnes & Noble Education, Inc.; Barnes & Noble College Booksellers, LLC; Follett Higher Education Group, Inc.; Educational Publishers Enforcement Group; In the United States District Court for the District of Delaware; Case 1:20-cv-00102-UNA. Kiyana Miller, individually and a representative of all others situated v. McGraw Global, LLC; Pearson Education, Inc.; Cengage Learning, Inc.; Barnes & Noble College Booksellers, LLC; Follett Higher Education Group, Inc.; Educational Publishers Enforcement Group; In the United States District Court District of New Jersey; Case 3:20-cv-07281. Elizabeth Kinskey and Grace Kinskey, individually and a representative of all others situated v. Barnes & Noble College Booksellers, LLC; Cengage Learning, Inc.; Follett Higher Education Group, Inc.; McGraw Global, LLC; Pearson Education, Inc.; United States District Court for the Southern District of Illinois; Case: 1:20-cv-02322. Martha Barabas, individually and a representative of all others situated v. McGraw Global, LLC; Pearson Education, Inc.; Cengage Learning, Inc.; Barnes & Noble College Booksellers, LLC; Barnes & College Booksellers, LLC; Cengage Learning, Inc.; Follett Higher Education Group, Inc.; McGraw-Hill Global Educational Holdings, LLC; Pearson Education, Inc. United States District Court for New Jersey; Case 3:20-cv-02442. Austan Warman, individually and a representative of all others situated v. Barnes & Noble College Booksellers, LLC; Barnes & College Booksellers, LLC; Cengage Learning, Inc.; Follett Higher Education Group, Inc.; McGraw-Hill Global Educational Holdings, LLC; Pearson Education, Inc. United States District Court for New Jersey; Case 3:20-cv-04875. The other suits were initiated by students in New Jersey individually and a representative of all others situated against the parties listed in the above New Jersey suits including Pica v. Barnes & Noble College Booksellers, LLC, et al.; Case No. 3:20-cv-04856; Puleo v. Barnes & Noble College Booksellers, LLC, et al; Case No. 3:20-cv-04990; Belen v. McGraw Hill, LLC, et al.; Case No. 3:20-cv-05394; Gordon, et al. v. Barnes & Noble College Booksellers, LLC, et al.; Case No. 3:20-cv-05535. Also in SDNY, Uchenik v. McGraw Hill, LLC, et al; Case No. 1:20-cv-03162.

53. Educational Publishers Enforcement Group, https://stopcounterfeitbooks.com/about/about-the-publishers. Also see R. Koenig. "Nine New Law Suits Target 'Inclusive Access' Textbook Programs, Alleging Antitrust Violations," https://www.edsurge.com/news/2020-05-21-nine-new-

lawsuits-target-inclusive-access-textbook-programs-alleging-antitrust-violations.

54. Cornell Law School. Law Information Institute. "The Sherman Act (15 U.S.C.)," https://www.law.cornell.edu/uscode/text/15/1; https://www.law.cornell.edu/uscode/text/15/2.

55. Cornell Law School. Law Information Institute. "The Clayton Act (15 U.S.C.)." https://www.law.cornell.edu/uscode/text/15/15; https://www.law.cornell.edu/uscode/text/15/26. The Federal Trade Commission. "The Antitrust Laws," www.ftc.gov/tips-advice/competition-guidance/guide-antitrust-laws/antitrust-laws.

56. United States Judicial Panel on Multidistrict Litigation. "In Re: Inclusive Access Course Materials Antitrust Litigation; Case: MDL: No. 2946." https://www.jpml.uscourts.gov/sites/jpml/files/MDL-2946-Transfer%20Order-7-20.pdf. Regarding the Southern District of New York, "The United States District Court for the Southern District of New York (SDNY) encompasses the counties of New York, Bronx, Westchester, Rockland, Putnam, Orange, Dutchess, and Sullivan and draws jurors from those counties. The Court hears cases in Manhattan, White Plains, and Poughkeepsie, New York;" https://www.nysd.uscourts.gov/about. Also see M. Leonard. "Online course materials monopolization cases centralized in N.Y.," https://news.bloomberglaw.com/antitrust/mcgraw-hill-b-n-accused-of-online-course-materials-monopoly.

57. United States District Court Southern District of New York. "In RE Inclusive Access Materials Antitrust Litigation. This File Related to 20cv6314. Master File No. 20 MDL No. 2946 (DLC). Consolidated Amended Class Action Complaint; Jury Trial Waived. Case 1:20-md-02946-DLC. Document No. 50. Filed 10/16/20."

58. *Ibid.*, p. 1.

59. *Ibid.*, p. 8.

60. *Ibid.*, pp. 11 and 25.

61. *Ibid.*, pp. 43–44

62. *Ibid.*, pp. 46–60, 69, 73–74.

63. *Ibid.*, pp. 79–80.

64. *Ibid.*, pp. 80–93.

65. United States Courts. "Federal Rules of Civil Procedure;" https://www.uscourts.gov/rules-policies/current-rules-practice-procedure/federal-rules-civil-procedure. The Federal Rules of Civil Procedure (effective as of Dec. 1, 2020) govern civil proceedings in the United States district courts. Their purpose is "to secure the just, speedy, and inexpensive determination of every action and proceeding." The rules were first adopted by order of the Supreme Court on December 20, 1937.

66. United States District Court Southern District of New York. "20 MDL No. 2946 (DLC). In re Inclusive Access Materials Antitrust Litig. Decided June 14, 2021. Denise Cote District Judge. Opinion and Order," https:// casetext.com/case/in-re-inclusive-access-course-materials-antitrust-litig.
67. *Ibid.*, pp. 2–8, 10, 13–14, 17, 19–20.
68. *Ibid.*, p. 21.
69. R. J. Krajick. Clerk of the Court. United States District Court Southern District of New York. "In Re: Inclusive Access Course Materials Antitrust Litigation. Case 1:20-md-02946-DLC. Judgment," https://www.courtlistener.com/docket/17433567/in-re-inclusive-access-course-materials-antitrust-litigation.
70. J. Stempel. "U.S. Judge Dismisses Antitrust Lawsuits Over College Textbooks," https://www.reuters.com/business/us-judge-dismisses-antitrust-lawsuit-over-college-textbooks-2021-06-14.

CHAPTER 5

The Future of College Textbook Publishing

Abstract It was apparent by 2022 and 2023 that the entire college text-book industry, publishers and bookstores, continued to have certain advantages. These included each publisher had carved out a formidable market position by releasing printed and digital texts in a wide variety of academic fields, and they continued to add new titles; all of the companies had modified their business models to develop (at some considerable cost) and emphasize the convenience, portability, student friendly features, the price of digital textbooks; major legal successes in the ReDigi and Inclusive Access cases; and deep interest in the Equitable Access program launched at UC Davis. Yet far too many structural weaknesses and threats remained that threatened the business of college textbook publishing, including financial instability and high debt of certain publishing firms; the ravages of the Covid pandemic; continued declines in both college enrollments and textbook sales; the impact of gender discrimination in the college textbook publishing sector; the impending threats of inflation and a possible recession; and the ever present threats posed by book pirates.

Keywords Risk in the college textbook industry • SWOT (strengths; weakness; opportunities; and threats) analysis of textbook publishing industry • Impact of Covid • Inclusive Access • Equitable Access • Gender discrimination in textbook publishing

© The Author(s), under exclusive license to Springer Nature Switzerland AG 2023
A. N. Greco, *The College Textbook Publishing Industry in the U.S. 2000–2022*, Marketing and Communication in Higher Education, https://doi.org/10.1007/978-3-031-30415-6_5

INTRODUCTION

Clearly, by the end of 2021, the level of business uncertainty and risk increased significantly for all of the higher education textbook publishers and bookstores. The *Merriam-Webster Dictionary* defined risk as "the possibility that something bad or unpleasant (such as an injury or a loss) will happen." Investopedia's definition of risk was more detailed. "In the financial world, risk management is the process of identification, analysis, and acceptance or mitigation of uncertainty in investment decisions. Essentially, risk management occurs when an investor or fund manager analyzes and attempts to quantify the potential for losses in an investment, such as a moral hazard, and then takes the appropriate action (or inaction) given the fund's investment objectives and risk tolerance."[1]

One approach to understand the level of risk all of the higher education textbook publishing (and college bookstore) companies face in the future (i.e., after 2021) was to undertake an analysis of the industry's strengths, weaknesses, opportunities, and threats, known as a SWOT analysis in business schools.

HIGHER EDUCATION TEXTBOOK PUBLISHERS' STRENGTHS

As for the strengths of the textbook publishing industry in the future, a review of the websites and reports issued by the publishers indicated conclusively that all of them exhibited the following. First, each publisher had carved out a formidable market position by releasing texts in a wide variety of academic fields, and they continued to add new titles as academic fields branched out into new sub-fields (known as "twigging"). Second, all of the companies had modified their business models to develop (at some considerable cost) and emphasize the convenience, portability, student friendly features (underlining, word search, etc.), and the price of digital textbooks.

Third, most of the large textbook firms developed important alliances, and book contracts, with well-known "star" academics who wrote "big" textbooks with large sell-through rates (e.g., economics). This strategy had been utilized effectively in the various creative industries for decades including trade books, for example, the great success of Mary Higgins Clark's adult trade fiction books; motion pictures, Alfred Hitchcock's large portfolio of very successful films; music, Ella Fitzgerald's decades of popular success and hit records; and live Broadway entertainment, Angela

Lansbury's ability to capture the attention of audiences over a long period of time. The fundamental belief was that a "star" brought intellectual and creative forces to a book, a film, a song, or any intellectual or creative endeavor generating ultimately positive cultural and commercial results. This theory was also the subject of a major article by Steven N. Kaplan, Berk A. Senroy, and Per Stromberg in the *Journal of Finance*. They asked the question about the importance of "stars." Should you bet (i.e., invest) on the "jockey" or the "horse"? So, which one was more important? Was it the "jockey" (i.e., the "star" with the creative idea and the ability to write a first rate book, make a film a global "blockbuster," or sing a piece of music) or the "horse" (i.e., the final product; the motion picture or the music and lyrics of a song)? Clearly, based on the data regarding textbook advances and multiple editions of successful texts, many if not all of the college textbook publishers "bet" on the "jockey," the author of the best-selling book, the "star;" however, Kaplan, et al., came to an opposite conclusion (they believed you should bet on the "horse") regarding venture capitalists and financing startup operations. But, then again, writing a successful college textbook is not the same as starting a new online dating website.[2]

Fourth, all of the major publishers had textbooks with U.S. copyright protection, and they had the support of the AAP to present their intellectual property concerns to the U.S. Congress, regulatory organizations, and key U.S. departments (e.g., the U.S. Department of Justice and the U.S. Department of Commerce). Fifth, revenue increases were posted by Pearson, Cengage, and the other three houses for the Spring (i.e., January to May) and Summer (i.e., June to August) 2021 semesters.[3] Sixth, Pearson, Cengage, Macmillan Academic, John Wily, and McGraw Hill all reported substantive increases in the transformation from a print to a digital oriented world. For example, Cengage sales in 2018 were 61% digital. By 2021, the percentages reached 73% digital, and by 2021, 100% of its titles were available as e-texts. Cengage reported that in 2021 digital text sale revenues increased 83% on 8.9 million digital units. So, the outlook for the digital transformation of the publishing companies, and a growing and clearly wider acceptance by students for e-texts, indicated strong growth potential for the years after 2021, with some very positive acceptance of digital textbooks projections out to 2026.[4] Seventh, the launch of the Inclusive Access (IA) strategy achieved noticeable successes, and impressive IA revenue tallies were posted by all five publishers.[5]

HIGHER EDUCATION TEXTBOOK PUBLISHERS' WEAKNESS

However, structural and business weaknesses were evident. First, many publishers had posted declines in revenues after 2014. This hampered the ability of most of the large textbook firms to increase cash reserves and develop needed operational performance results. In essence, too many of them struggled to increase their return on invested capital (ROIC), an exceptionally important financial metric for stockholders and the financial service companies (e.g., Morgan Stanley; Goldman Sachs). Second, three of the publishing companies (e.g., McGraw Hill; Cengage; and John Wiley) wanted to "get big" by relying on an organic growth strategy (i.e., growing the company internally by increasing textbook output, sales, market share, and profit margins rather than utilizing mergers and acquisitions). However, their emphasis on a "winner-take-all" market share strategy was ultimately counter-productive. A more successful strategy would have been to increase the entire market for textbooks, in essence to have more college textbook revenues for all of the houses, a strategy emphasized by Michael Porter.[6]

Third, the Covid lockdowns and the closing of colleges by March 2020 limited significantly the efforts of the publishers to reach faculty members. Faculty offices were closed. Academic conferences either were canceled or went virtual in the Spring of 2020, and this extended into 2021 and, in some instances, into 2022. Sales representatives relied on Zoom meetings, emails, and telephone calls to inform faculty members of new texts or new editions of an existing book. The only "possibly positive" result of this situation was the fact that all of the college textbook publishers saved hundreds of thousands of dollars in marketing expenses, including costs for booths (in reality tables) at academic conferences, and transportation, hotel, and per diem fees to send reps to the conferences or to visit colleges. These financial savings, as one publisher stated in an interview, went right to the bottom line. Fourth, the textbook business remained vulnerable when substitute products (i.e., rental and used texts) challenged their financial position in the marketplace. Fifth, a few of the publishing operations looked outside the world of book publishing for chief executive officers (CEOs). This reliance on the well-established business school concept that an effective manager could manage any operation, 1 day managing a jet engine manufacturing faculty and the next day running a book publishing firm, was, at best, an interesting theory and, at worst, intellectually shallow and a flawed theory. Running a college textbook company is clearly not the same as, for example, managing a strategic business unit at General Electric or running a hedge fund.

HIGHER EDUCATION TEXTBOOK PUBLISHERS' OPPORTUNITIES

Opportunities after 2021 were abundant but, too frequently, difficult to achieve. First, a merger or acquisition can enable a publisher to obtain book titles, author contracts, market share, effective sales reps, and revenues. The failure of McGraw Hill and Cengage to merge triggered the sale of McGraw Hill in 2021. The company was sold by Apollo to Platium Equity. Platium Equity, a diversified American company, had $19 billion in assets under management (AUM) in 2021.[7] However, it is possible that "small" mergers and acquisitions could occur and receive approval from the anti-trust division at either the Department of Justice (DOJ) or the Federal Trade Commission (FTC), and an acquisition outside of textbook publishing, perhaps buying a warehouse (to increase a firm's logistics capabilities) or an accounting software company to handle accounts payable and receivables (e.g., to manage more effectively cash flow) could pass muster at DOJ or FTC. Second, the return to in-person classes in the Fall of 2021 should generate ultimately some positive increases in the sale of textbooks, LMS systems, and corporate profits.

Third, IA should reduce the threats posed by the pervasive online used and rental sites, provide a student with the text before or on the first day of class at reduced SRPs, and increase "sell-through rates." Fourth, the disintermediation strategy of selling directly to students (known as D-2-C) should or could generate sales and, perhaps more importantly, a plethora of student user data that could assist a publishing company in becoming more innovative, data-driven, managed, profitable, and, hopefully, better prepared for the next economic downturn.[8] In essence, they can focus effectively on tracking the unique way supply and demand operates in the textbook business as well as end-user satisfaction indicators. They can create adaptive marketing budgets and build flexibility into the firm's supply chains. This means that the publishers should reevaluate the belief that they can anticipate or determine specific outcomes and, instead, concentrate their efforts to measure and understand student demand as it arises. A related benefit could enable publishers to move away from the "80%–20% Pareto Power Law" world (i.e., 80% of a firm's revenues come from 20%

of its titles) into a business climate were a larger percentage of titles in the firm's textbook portfolio generate a profit.

Fifth, the publishers learned some important things during this Covid lockdown and Zoom classroom environment regarding better ways to reach faculty members about their new texts, and they need to use this knowledge to make better decisions in the future. Sixth, the publishers need to determine more precisely what educational resources faculty members want for their students. Seventh, the possibility exists of working more successfully with academic libraries to license e-textbooks for student use.

Eighth, textbook publishers could create some innovative strategies to offer more value to students. For example, in 2021 Pearson, cutting through the "Gordian knot" of market uncertainty and building on its largest market share in the college textbook industry, launched "Pearson+ a new subscription based learning experience" for students. In essence, "Pearson+" was a rental D-2-C access program that gave college students a flexible, affordable access to +1500 Pearson digital textbooks and study tools, flashcards, and audio (for selected titles). The company offered a two-tiered bundle subscription pricing option. Access to a single title (the "single-tier") was $9.99 a month (for a 4 month subscription), and the "multi-tier" option was $14.99 a month (also for 4 months), providing a student with access to +1500 Pearson college textbooks in an "all you can eat" option. This meant that a student using "Pearson+" was free to select exactly what he or she needed utilizing a monthly subscription fee rather than a single up-front payment option. Pearson also offered faculty members access to "syllabus support" to make this a "seamless" offering. "Pearson+" could be a game changer, a "Netflix" type streaming textbook on demand (TOB) option. The technological options were significant since "Pearson+" was available on a student's desktop, laptop, and a mobile app; it provided 24/7 student access management and support system; and the company used a PayPal payment option. Since Pearson published so many "big textbooks" in a wide variety of academic fields, the multi-tier option could be very attractive economically to students using more than one Pearson book. However, there could be concerns raised by Pearson authors. The traditional royalty payment was a "back-end" profit participation system, and royalties could be calculated based on the number of net units sold to students. In an "all you can eat" access system, ascertaining royalty payment for a specific title in a sea of +1500 textbooks could be challenging even for a company with sophisticated analytical operations.[9]

Higher Education Textbook Publishers' Threats

The number of threats increased dramatically in the years after 2000 and continued past 2021 and into 2022 and 2023. First, competition between the publishers increased exponentially, possibly cutting into margins. Second, the debt level of certain college textbook publishing firms bordered on the unsustainable. McGraw Hill reported in their annual report that, as of March 2021, their debt level exceeded $2 billion; Cengage's debt in 2021 stood at $1.77 billion.[10] Third, the open access (OA) and open educational resources (OER) programs are free substitute products, and they will not disappear from, and could gain more traction in, the academic landscape, hurting the sales of the big publishers.

Fourth, any decrease in the number of U.S. non-profit colleges could impact adversely print or digital textbook sales. Between academic years 2017–2018 and 2020–2021, the U.S. Department of Education's NCES reported a decline in the number of private non-profit four year institutions (from 1643 in 2017–2018 to 1608 in 2020–2021, -2.13%); public non-profit two-year colleges posted declines, during those same years from 2017–2018 to 2020–2021, from 978 to 920, -5.93%); and private non-profit two-year colleges went from 159 to 139, -12.58%).[11] Table 5.1 has the enrollments projections from the U.S. Department of Education for 2022 through 2028.

Fifth, it is likely that printed textbooks will be used by many students for the next few years (i.e., the "average" hard cover textbook with "normal wear" and with a sewn Smythe binding can have 5–7 "turns;" in essence a text could be resold up to 7 times). Also, since a large percentage of textbooks are printed abroad and imported into the U.S., publishers have experienced both an increase in costs and serious service disruptions in the printed book supply chain. Clearly, this could be a real threat in supplying textbooks to students in the next few years.[12] In addition, the impact of inflation and economic uncertainty (and a possible recession) remained a concern for every publisher in 2021, 2022, and especially in 2023.

Sixth, starting sometime in March 2020, the majority of (if not every) textbook publishers closed offices and relied on employees working remotely. Concerns have been expressed by many publishers about the

Table 5.1 Total U.S. non-profit public and private college students, 2022–2028

Year	Undergraduate and graduate students			Total annual
	Full-time	Part-time	Total	Percentage change
2022	12,131,000	7,860,000	19,991,000	+0.18%
2023	12,145,000	7,895,000	20,040,000	+0.25%
2024	12,178,000	7,929,000	20,107,000	+0.33%
2025	12,220,000	7,557,000	20,177,000	+0.35%
2026	12,264,000	7,994,000	20,258,000	+0.40%
2027	12,272,000	8,023,000	20,295,000	+0.18%
2028	12,261,000	8,044,000	20,305,000	+0.05%
Percent Change 2022–2028	+1.07%	+2.34%	+1.57%	–

Source: U.S. Department of Education. National Center for Education Statistics, https://nces.ed.gov/programs/digest/d18/tables/dt18_303.10.asp

N.B. All numbers were rounded off and may not always equal 100 percent. Education estimates

difficulties and expenses of office renovations (e.g., installing more efficient air circulating systems, maintaining sanitary conference rooms, break-out rooms, etc.) when employees returned to publishing offices. A second and more important issue was whether some employees, especially in the creative operations (e.g., editors, art and design personnel, etc.) and sales and marketing, might not want to return to a traditional cubicle-oriented office since remote working seemed to be successful. A third employee issue related to safety concerns about using mass transit systems to get to an office (especially the New York City subway and bus systems or train or bus travel to and from New York City's Grand Central Station or Penn Station).

Seventh, data released by AAP indicated that net publisher's revenues stood at only $3.22 billion in 2021. AAP also released textbook revenue data for July 2021 through July 2022 and college course materials declined to -19.8% between July 2021 and July 2022; in addition, AAP reported that college textbook revenues were down to -9.1% for the first 7 months of 2022 when compared to that same period in 2021.[13] Compounding these revenue declines was a report in *The Wall Street Journal* that "college enrollments declined for the third consecutive school year… dropping 1.1% [in the fall 2022 semester] since last [i.e., 2021] Autumn. Over the first 2 years of the Covid-19 pandemic, [college] enrollments fell about 6.5%, according to the National Student Clearinghouse... About 1.5 million fewer students are enrolled in college than before the pandemic..."[14].

OTHER MAJOR UNRESOLVED CONCERNS: INTELLECTUAL PROPERTY ISSUES

Book publishers were very concerned with the Kirtsaeng decision; however, they were pleased with the ReDigi and Inclusive Access legal decisions. However, enforcement of copyright infringements remained a serious problem for every part of the U.S. book industry including the college textbook sector. This issue was addressed specifically by Stephen E. Siwek, for the International Intellectual Property Alliance (IIPA),[15] and Digimarc in their study "Inside the Mind of a Book Pirate," which indicated that U.S. book publishers lost about $300 million annually in book piracy (and this was only a rough estimate of total losses).[16] Actually losses by higher education publishers were not addressed specifically by Siwek or Digimarc. However, discussions with college textbook executives and various retailers indicated clearly that there were sizable financial losses by the textbook publisher sector, especially in the used, rental, and piracy textbook sector (possibly $1 billion).

While the AAP has been vigilant in monitoring piracy sites, the AAP believed that book piracy, including the piracy of college textbooks, increased significantly in the years after 2012 because of the wide acceptance of digital technologies, posing yet another major threat to the incomes of authors, publishers, and college bookstores.

OTHER MAJOR UNRESOLVED CONCERNS: GENDER DISCRIMINATION IN COLLEGE TEXTBOOK PUBLISHING AND AUTHORSHIP

The closing of universities, libraries, and major archives had a deleterious impact on academic researchers. Research projects, laboratory experiments, the "temporary closing" of many doctoral programs, and travel to conferences stopped rather abruptly, and this had an impact on book (including college textbook) and journal research.[17] A number of major research studies indicated clearly that female academics, often with major family responsibilities, were compelled to modify or postpone scholarly research during the Covid lockdown.[18] However, gender disparity issues in scholarly research predates the Covid situation, especially in the eclectic scientific, technical, and medical (STM) research journal fields.

This STM journal situation was addressed in a series of major scholarly studies, including the research of Anna Fazackerley ("Women's Research Plummets During Lockdown—But Articles from Men Increase"); Natalie Grover ("Papers by Women Have Fewer Citations in Top Medical Journals-Study"); Janice Hopkins Tanne ("White Male Authors Still Dominate Top Academic Medical Journals, Two Studies Report"); Matthew B. Ross, Britta M. Glennon, Raviv Murciano-Goroff, Erica G. Berkes, Bruce A. Weinberg, and Julia I. Lane ("Women Are Credited Less in Science Than Are Men"); Yiqin Alicia Shen, Jason M. Webster, Yuichi Shoda, and Ione Fine ("Persistent Underrepresentation of Women's Science in High Profile Journals"); and Goran Muric, Kristina Lerman, and Emilio Ferrara ("Gender Disparity in the Authorship of Biomedical Research Publications During the Covid-19 Pandemic: Retrospective Observational Study").[19]

However, gender disparity issues were also very evident in the college textbook sector. Betsey Stevenson wrote that "economics remains dominated by men, both in terms of faculty members and students. New research suggests that while economics textbooks are not necessarily to blame, they are not helping close the field's gender gap. A study of leading introductory economics textbooks, presented last week at the annual meeting of the American Economic Association [AEA], found that three-quarters of the people mentioned in the books real or imagined, are male..."[20] This pattern was also evident in political science-American government textbooks. Christiane Olivio wrote that research about 12 leading introductory American government and politics textbooks revealed "their main narratives still focus largely on men's experiences as political actors and pay little attention to women's experiences."[21] Amy L. Atchinson wrote that "the extant literature indicates that gender is not well represented in American government textbooks, thus signaling to students that women and gender are not part of the mainstream in political science."[22] Jessica Lavariega Monforti and Adam McGlynn reviewed 29 introductory U.S. government and political science textbooks. They wrote that these texts "[ignore] the political experiences and influences of racial, ethnic and other minority groups... [we] access the level of coverage and treatment of Latinos/as, the fastest growing racial/ethnic group in the country. We find that the discussion of Latinos in these textbooks is incredibly brief and often limited to the civil rights chapters… [and] their overall contributions to the political development of the United States is largely ignored."[23]

The STM textbook field was also analyzed in a number of major research studies. Sara Wood, Jeremiah A. Henning, Luoying Chen, Taylor McKibben, Michael L. Smith, Majorie Weber, Ash Zemenick, and Cissy J. Ballen investigated biology textbooks. They insisted that "the scientists portrayed in [biology] textbooks are not representative of their target audience—the student population. Overall, very few scientists of color were highlighted, and projections suggest it could take multiple centuries at current rates before we reach inclusive representation. We call upon textbook publishers to expand upon the scientists they highlight to reflect diverse populations of learners in biology."[24]

Chemistry textbooks also exhibited similar patterns of gender discrimination. Laura Norton and Ale Palermo wrote that "whilst we have made some progress in response to improve equality, diversity, and inclusion in the chemical sciences in relation to gender, there is still a long way to go. Today, chemistry does not yet welcome everyone—but it should."[25] Racial representation issues in chemistry texts was also addressed by Claire L. Jarvis. She wrote that "the [chemistry] textbooks that thousands of students read each year still lag. White men predominate in the images and references to historical science figures. Many publishers are starting to implement changes to improve racial and gender diversity within their pages, but progress is slow."[26] Mona L. Becker and Melanie R. Nilsson studied "gender representation in 10 current [2016–2020] U.S. college-level general chemistry textbooks. On average, females were found to constitute 30% of images and 3% of the named science, technology, engineering, math, and medical (STEMM) professionals in the index… Gender imbalance was ubiquitous among all publishers examined… We speculate that male overrepresentation in chemistry textbooks reflects and perpetuates unconscious gender bias in STEMM."[27]

Timothy M. Lawler and Timothy Niiler addressed physics textbooks published between 1960 and 2016, and they observed both gender and racial bias in the texts. "We find that the distribution of images in 11 physics textbooks over a wide range of years is not favorable to women and ethnic or racial minorities."[28]

These research studies and concerns did capture the attention of many if not most textbook publishers. Lindsay McKenzie reported that "Pearson yesterday [i.e., February 25, 2021] published editorial guidelines addressing race, ethnicity, equity, and inclusion, becoming one of the first major textbook publishers to make such guidelines publicly available."[29] However, the entire textbook publishing industry needs to address these gender and discrimination issues if they hope to remain a relevant part of society and the academic community.

OTHER MAJOR UNRESOLVED CONCERNS: TEXTBOOK PUBLISHERS AND COLLEGE BOOKSTORES CONFRONT ECONOMIC UNCERTAINTY

In 2022 and into 2023, major concerns about the impact of inflation, and the possibility that the U.S. might enter a recession, dominated financial reporting, including articles and reports in *The Wall Street Journal* (*WSJ*), the University of Michigan's [Michigan] "Survey of Consumer," and *Publishers Weekly (PW)*.

Amara Omeokwe reported in May 2022 in the *WSJ* that the Congressional Budget Office (CBO) "projects inflation, economic growth to cool this year [2022] and next [2023]... [and] the Federal Reserve has begun raising interest rates in an effort to combat inflation..."[30] The Michigan report in May 2022 stated that "consumer sentiment, which fell 10.4% below April [2022]... was largely driven by continued negative views on current buying conditions for houses and durables, as well as consumers' future outlook for the economy, primarily due to concerns over inflation."[31] Greg Ip in the *WSJ* in June 2022 wrote that "inflation at the end of last year [2021] was more than double the median projections among economists surveyed 8 months earlier and well above the highest forecast." Ip observed that economists have long used various econometric models to predict inflation. Unfortunately, "these models worked reasonably well over the roughly 40 years before the Covid-19 pandemic, but not since. 'Economists do not have a satisfactory theory of inflation at this point,' said Harvard University's Larry Summers."[32] By late June 2022, Harriet Torry and Anthony DeBarros reported that "economists say recession is likelier;" an observation also written about in the *WSJ* by Bryan Mena.[33]

Larry Summers, a former U.S. Secretary of the Treasury, emerged as a leading expert about the economic uncertainty evident in the U.S.[34] James Mackintosh, also in the *WSJ* in June 2022, conceded that Summers was correct, and Mackintosh was wrong, in February 2022 regarding signs that increased inflation would be a major problem.[35] *The New Yorker's* John Cassidy supported Summers' view that "there is about a one-third chance that inflation will significantly accelerate over the next several years."[36]

By June 2022, Rina Torchinsky, also in the *WSJ*, wrote that "consumers' short-term outlook for the U.S. economy dropped sharply in its lowest point in nearly a decade on concerns about inflation, the Conference Board consumer-confidence survey showed."[37] The *WSJ's* reporters in July 2022 addressed the economic malaise evident in the U.S. Jon Hilsenrath wondered "if the U.S. is in a recession, it's a very strange one…Economic output fell in the first quarter and signs suggest it did so again in the second. Yet the job market showed little signs of faltering during the first half of the year."[38] Brian Whitton wrote that "in June, the consumer-price index rose 9.1% from the year before… surging energy costs, along with staffing challenges and labor costs, have been driving up housing, groceries, lawn care, even haircuts." Yet he asked when will prices stop going up?[39] By August 2022, Paul Hannon reported that "business activity in the U.S., Europe, and Japan fell in August… pointing to a sharp slowdown in global economic growth… U.S. companies reported a sharp drop in business activity in August [2022] in a broad-based decline led by service companies, though manufacturing slowed as well."[40] In the days just before Labor Day 2022, Nick Timiraos addressed this dilemma in the U.S. "What if the drivers of inflation are here to stay?"[41].

Clearly, the entire U.S. book publishing industry was impacted by inflation and concerns about what a recession could do to book sales. Jim Milliot and his associates at *PW* surveyed the publishing landscape in 2022 stressing the impact of supply chain problems and costs. In February, Milliot reported that "the impact of supply chain disruptions and higher costs on publishers' earnings is starting to come into focus…"[42] Ed Nawotka in May 2022 observed that "troubles with the supply chain persist. Problems include a shortage of materials, increased freight prices, and port congestion [i.e., the importation of books, including textbooks, mainly from Asia]. All of this is putting a strain on publishers as it becomes more difficult for them to accurately predict demand, consequently, to supply a given title."[43]

Unfortunately, the AAP's data underscored the concerns of certain publishers and bookstores in 2022. Barnes & Noble Education reported net losses for the fiscal year (FY) ending on April 30, 2022.[44] Pearson reported a -6.55% decline in U.S. revenues in 2022. College textbook declines were reported by Cengage, McGraw Hill, and Wiley.[45]

A New Option for College Textbook Publishers and Bookstores: Equitable Access

By December 2022, more than 1000 colleges offered the Inclusive Access (IA) option (sometimes called "First Day" for some publishers) for students, and it has proven to be rather successful. In the Fall of 2020, the University of California, Davis (Davis) launched an innovative pilot program which was in reality a "significantly modified" version of IA called "Equitable Access" (EA), and a student could "opt-out" of the EA program as they could in IA. Davis is on a quarter semester system not a semester system.[46]

The basic terms and conditions of Davis's EA program gave "students digital access to course materials for a quarterly flat fee, payable with financial aid, tentatively set at $199. It aims to address inequality from various textbook costs... Equitable Access will be available to all undergraduates... 'The program levels the playing field,' said Aleasha Jhanjar a fourth-year psychology major."[47] Davis was able to reduce the EA fee from $199 to $169 per quarter, and both printed and digital educational materials were available through EA.[48]

This meant that, for example, an undergraduate pre-medicine student at UC Davis might take three courses in a Fall quarter semester, possibly: *Campbell Biology, 12th edition* (Pearson; the suggested retail price for this hardcover text was $597.08 according to the Fall 2022 publisher's website); Stewart's *Calculus: Single Variable Calculus Early Transcendentals* (Cengage; the hardcover SRP was $274.95), and Brown, et al. *Chemistry: The Central Science, 15th edition* (Pearson; hardcover SRP was $319.99). The suggested retail prices (SRPs) for these three new hard cover textbooks (as indicated on the Cengage and Pearson publisher's website) was $1192.02. However, the Davis pre-med student paid $169.00 for the hardcover printed and/or digital versions of these textbooks (a saving of $1023.02). Of course, in the U.S. a college bookstore can charge whatever its wants for a text, either higher or lower than the publisher's SRP.

The Davis EA plan generated a great deal of positive publicity. Bill Rosenblatt wrote that the Davis EA program was "to inject predictability into textbook pricing so that students pay more or less for each course, regardless of subject or major." Rosenblatt outlined why publishers would agree to reduce the SRP for a text. "The basic bargain for publishers is this: US Davis will guarantee publishers up to a fixed amount of money—currently envisioned at $20—for every student in every class that adopts one of the publisher's books."[49]

The National Association of College Stores (NACS) described how Davis was able to launch EA. "It took 2 years for US Davis to reach this point [of launching EA] because much of the work involved negotiations with the 12 largest textbook publishers, all of whom are now on board [i.e., as of December 2020] with the program... Gaining student buy-in was also important."[50] Goldie Blumenstyk compared the UC Davis EA program to a "health insurance model." "If that [i.e., the Davis EA program] sounds a little like the way health insurance works..., it's no accident. Jason Lorgan, the US Davis official who is the architect of the idea, says both markets suffer from the same 'principal-agent problem.' That's when the person assigning a book (or prescribing a medicine) isn't the one paying for it... The 'equitable access' business approach carries other risks. If professors require books that are not covered by whatever deals UC Davis cuts with publishers, that could add expenses to the program. Or as Lorgan puts it, 'that's sort of like our flu epidemic."[51] VitalSource emerged as a major partner with the Davis EA program. "UC Davis wanted to provide a solution to the unpredictable cost of course materials and help alleviate financial barriers that can prevent students from pursuing their learning goals. The team at VitalSource was honored to work with UC Davis to build this program."[52]

Robert Jansen outlined the 10 best practices for an Equitable Access program, including working closely with NACS and ensuring that a clear opt-out policy existed.[53] Other colleges paid attention to the Davis experience, as well as suggestions regarding launching and maintaining an effective EA program. For example, San Diego State's EA program went into effect in the Fall 2022 semester.[54]

EA does address textbooks costs, and students can opt-out of EA. However, some students might compare the basic EA amount charged at Davis or San Diego State for educational materials versus the costs to buy used or rental copies of textbooks, the same issue raised by many of the plaintiffs in the Inclusive Access cases. For example, the rental costs for hardcover copies of the three science textbooks listed above (i.e., at UC Davis) in September 2022 are as follows: Campbell $74.99, Stewart $65.07, and Brown $35.45, for a total of $175.51. Davis charged the student $169 for these three books, so the student saved $6.51. Clearly, EA is still an exceptionally intriguing "work in progress."

CONCLUSION: COMMENTS ON THE FUTURE

"It's tough to make predictions, especially about the future."[55]
Yogi Berra (Baseball Hall of Fame).

Predicting the future has long been an area of interest and concern to academic researchers in economics, marketing, finance, and in other fields, but, too often, predictions fail and end up in the dust-bin of history. Several pivotal facts are known that might help college textbook publishers confront their future. First, in light of past events, the entire higher education textbook publishing sector will confront serious, vexing problems and, for some publishers, financial and business uncertainty in the coming years, and the tireless quest to get "big" just might turn out to be a hollow strategy. Second, there is the harsh, brutal fact that the college textbook business has changed since 2000, and it will never be the same as it was in the past. As Heraclitus said, "the only thing that is constant is change."[56]

The smart, effective executives running textbook publishing will grasp these facts, and they will address the inevitable changes and threats they will face in the coming years. Those who do not face the realities of the current state of higher education publishing, specifically executives who are "drawn back ceaselessly into the past,"[57] could fail. This is how the college textbook business has worked since that fateful day in 1478 when the Oxford University Press opened its doors and printed and published its first book used in classroom instruction.

NOTES

1. Merriam-Webster Dictionary. "Risk," www.merriam-webster.com/dictionary/risk. Also see Investopedia. "Risk Management in Finance," www.merriam-webster.com/dictionary/risk.
2. S.N. Kaplan, B.A. Sensoy, P. Stromberg. "Should Investors Bet on the Jockey or the Horse? Evidence From the Evolution of Firms From Early Business Plans to Public Companies," *Journal of Finance*, 64, 1(February 2009), 75–115. Also see I.C. Macmillan, R. Siegel, P.N. Subba Narashimha. "Criteria Used by Venture Capitalists to Evaluate New Venture Proposals,"

Journal of Business Venturing, 1, 1(Winter 1985), 119–128. H. Vogel. *Entertainment Industry Economics: A Guide for Financial Analysis, 4th edition,* pp. 22–27. C. Jones, M. Lorenzen, J. Sapsed. "Creative Industries: A Typology of Change," in C. Jones, M. Lorenzen, J. Sapsed (eds), *The Oxford Handbook of Creative Industries* (Oxford: Oxford University Press, 2015), pp. 3–30.

3. Cengage Learning Holdings II, Inc. "Third Quarter Report: Three and Nine Months Ended December 31, 2020," cengage.widen.net/content/feyqmvrdoa/pdf/Fiscal-year-2021-Third-Quarter-December-31-2020.pdf?u-fn2gt2. McGraw Hill. "Preliminary Fiscal Q4 & FY 2021 Investor Update," s22.q4cdn.com/942918855/files/doc_news/2021-Q4/Final. John Wiley & Sons, Inc. "Third Quarter 2021 Earnings Report," wiley-ecomm-good-content.s3.amazonaws.com/Q321_Earnings_Presentation.pdf.

4. C. Francis. "Digital Educational Publishing Market to Witness Huge Growth," manometcurrent.com/digital-educational-publishing-market-to-witness-huge-growth-by-2026-Hachette-livre-mcgraw-hill-education-holtzbrinck-publishing-growth- by-2026.

5. J.R. Young, "Colleges Are Striking Bulk Deals with Textbook Publishers. Critics Say There Are Many Downsides," www.edsurge.com/news/2019-05-23-colleges-are-striking-bulk-deals-with-textbook-publishers-critics-say-there-are-many-downsides. Also see A. Hess. "7 Ways the Coronavirus Pandemic Could Change College This Fall," www.cnbc.com/2020/06/19/7-ways-coronavirus-pandemic-may-change-college-this-fall-and-forever.html.

6. R.H. Thaler. *The Winner's Curse: Paradoxes and Anomalies of Economic Life* (Princeton: Princeton University Press, 1994), pp. 50–78. Also see R.H. Frank, P.J. Cook. *The Winner-take-All Society: Why the Few at the Top Get so Much More Than the Rest of Us* (New York: Penguin Books, 1996), pp. 1–44, 189–210. J.K. Galbraith, "The winner Takes All… Sometimes," hbr.org/1995/11/the-winner-takes-all-sometimes.

7. M. Gottfried. "Platium Equity Strikes Deal to Buy McGraw Hill from Apollo," www.wsj.com/articles/platium-equity-strikes-deal-to-buy-msgraw-hill-from-apollo-11623788101. Also see Platium Equity. 'Platium Equity News,' www.platinumequity.com/news/news-articles/2020/10-billion-dollar-fund-v,

8. V. Meyer-Schonberger, T. Ramge. "Are the Most Innovative Companies Just the Ones With the Most Data?" HBR.org/2018/02/are-the-most-innovative-companies-just-the-ones-with-yje-most-data.   Also see R. Wartzman, L. Crosby. "With the Best-Managed Companies, Bigger May Mean Better," *The Wall Street Journal,* April 14, 1919, 14. M. Reeves, K. Whitaker, C. Ketels. "Companies Need to Prepare for the

Next Economic Downturn," hbr.org/2019/04/companies-need-to-prepare-for-the next-economic-downturn?utm_medium-email- finance_not_activesubs&referral-00209&deliveryName=DM34889.

9. Pearson Higher Ed. "Big News—Introducing Pearson+," mail.google.com/mail/u/1/?ogbl#inbox/FMfcgzGkZkLrdhvZcTgLDQHWqxdmwPTp. Also see Pearson. "Interim Results for the Six Months to 30th June 2021," C:/Users.angre/Downloads/1495739.pdf. A. Prang. "Beyond Textbooks: Pearson PLC's CEO Andy Bird on How the Publisher Is Betting That Virtual Learning Is Going to Keep Growing After the Pandemic Ends," *The Wall Street Journal*, August 2, 2021, R2. R. Anderson. "Pearson Launches A Comprehensive Textbook Solution for Students. What Are Its Prospects?" scholarlykitchen.sspnet.org/2021/08/02/pearson=launches-a-comprehensive-textbook-solution-for-students-what-are-its-prospects/?informz=1. Pearson. "Introducing Pearson+: The Most Student and Budget Friendly College Learning Experience,' plc.pearson.com/en-GB/news/introducing-pearson-most-student-and-budget-friendly-college-learning-experience. Pearson. "Help Center: Account Management," www.pearson.com/en-us/pearsonplus/support/account-management.html. Pearson. "Help Center: Payments," www.pearson.com/en-us/pearsonplus/support/payments.html.

10. McGraw Hill. "McGraw-Hill Education, Inc., Annual Report as of March 31, 2021, and 2020," s22.q4cdn.com/942918855/files/doc_financials/2021/ar/MHE-2021.03.31-Annual-Report-Final.pdf. Also see Cengage Learning. "Investor Update June 17, 2021," Cengage-FY21-Q4-YE-Investor-Update-June-17-2021-Final.pdf. Also see KPMG. "Economic Growth In A Time of Disequilibrium: Examining Supply and Demand Imbalances caused by Covid-19," home.kpmg/xx/en/home/insights/2021/02/2021-macroeconomic-outlook.html.

11. U.S. Department of Education. National Center for Education Statistics, "Number of Title IV Institutions," nces.ed.gov/ipeds/search?querry-&query2=&resuitType=table&page=1&sortBy=date_desc&surveyComponents=12-month%20Enrollment%20(E12)&surveyComponents=Completions%20(C)&surveyComponents=Institutionall%20Characteristics%20(IC)&collectionYears=2020–21%sources=Tables%20Library&overlayTableld=25,207. Also see C. Guren, T. McIlroy, S. Sieck. "Covid-10 and Book Publishing Impacts and Insights, for 2021," *Publishing Research Quarterly*, https://doi.org/10.1007/s12109-021-09791-z.

12. J. Milliot. "High Costs, Service Disruptions Plague Book Biz Supply Chain," www.publishersweekly.com/paper-copy/by-topic/industry-news/manufacturing/article/86833-high-costs-services-disruptions-plague-book-biz-supply-chain.html. Also see T. McIlroy. "The Impact of

Recessions on Publishing Industries, Part III: Books," thefutureofpublishing.com/2019/04/the-impact-of-recessions-on-publishing-industries-part-iii-books.

13. J. Milliot. "2021 Was A Stellar Year for Publishing," https://www.publishersweekly.com/pw/by-topic/industry=news/publisher-news/article/90440-221-was-a stellar-year-for-oublishing.html. Also see Association of American Publishers (AAP). AAP July 2022 StatShot Report: Publishing Industry Down 4.1% Year-to-Year and Down 14.9% for July," https://publishers.org/news/aap-july-2022-statshot-report-publishing-industry-down-4-1-year-to-date-and-down-14-9-for-july.

14. D. Belkin. "College Enrollment Declines Again Through Online Schools, HBCUs See Increases," https://www.wsj.com/articles/college-enrollment-declines-again-through-online-schools-HBCUs-see-increases-11666223613?mod=hp_lead_pos11.

15. S.E. Stiwek. "Copyright Industries in the U.S. Economy: The 2013 Report," www.iipa.org/files/uploads/2018/01/2013CpyrtRptFull.pdf.

16. Digimarc. "Inside the Mind of A Book Pirate," www.digimarc.com/resources/ebook-piracy-study. Also see A. Lakkaraju. "Opinion: Textbook Piracy is Morally Justified," https://dailyillini.com/opinions-stodies/2022/08/31/textbook-piracy-college.

17. M. Korn. "Pandemic Leads Dozens of Universities to Pause Ph.D. admissions," www.wsj.com/articles/pandemic-leads-dozens-of-universities-to-pause-ph-d-admissions-11609261200.

18. G. Viglione. "Are Women Publishing Less During the Pandemic? Here's What the Data Shows," www.nature.com/articles/d41586-020-01294-9. Also see W. Reynolds. "Gender Disparity in Publishing May Be Widening for Physicians due to Covid-19," https://news.northwestern.edu/stories/2022/01/covid-gender-gap. A.K. Ribarovska, M.R. Hutchinson, Q.J. Pittman, C. Pariante, S.J. Spencer. "Gender Inequality in Publishing During Covid-19 Pandemic," https://doi.org/10.1016/j.bbi.2020.11.022. D. Jemielniak, A. Stawska, M. Wilamowski. "Covid-19 Effect on the Gender Gap in Academic Publishing," https://doi.org/10.1177/01655515211068168.

19. A. Fazackerley. "Women's Research Plummets During Lockdown-But Articles From Men Increase," https://www.theguardian.com/education/2020/may/12/womens'research-plummets-during-lockdown-but-articles-from-men-increase. Also see N. Grover. "Papers by Women Have Fewer Citations in Top Medical Journals-Study," https://www.theguardian.com/science/2021/jul/02/papers-by-women-have-fewer-citations-in-top-medical-journalsld-study. J. H. Tanne. "White Male Authors Still Dominate Top Academic Medical Publications, Two Studies Report," https://www.bmj.com/content/377/bmj.

o1044. M.B. Ross, B.M. Glennon, R. Murciano-Goroff, E.G. Berkes, B.A. Weinberg, J.I. Lane. "Women Are Credited Less in Science Than Are Men," https://www.nature.com/articles/s41586-022-04966-w. Y.A. Shen, J.M. Webster, Y.Shoda, I. Fine. "Persistent Underrepresentation of Women's Science in High Profile Journals," https://www.biorxiv.org/content/10.1101/275362v2. G. Muric, K. Lerman, E. Ferrara. "Gender Disparity in the Authorship of Biomedical Research Publications During the Covid-19 Pandemic: Retrospective Observational Study," http://www.jmir.org/2021/4/e25379.

20. B. Stevenson. "Gender Bias by the Numbers," https://www.insidehighered.com/news/2018/01/19/women-are-underrepresented-economics-textbooks-says-new-analysis-implications-fields. Also see S. Hagemann. "Why Does Gender Inequality in Academic Publishing Persist? Lessons and Recommendations," https://doi:org10.1177/14651165221120773. O. Kilic. "Do Women Have More barriers for Professional Development?" *European Psychiatry*, https://doi.org/10.1192/j.eurpsy.2022.199.

21. C. Olivo. "Bringing Women In: Gender and American Government and Politics Textbooks," https://doi.org/10.1080/15512169.2012.667676. Also see A.L. Mathews, K. Andersen. "A Gender Gap in Publishing? Women's representation in Edited Political Science Books," *PS: Political Science and Politics, 34*, 1 (Match 2001); 143–147. J.M. Krebsbach. "Women in Academia: Representation, Tenure, and Publication Patterns in the STEM and Social sciences Fields," https://vc.bridgew.edu/jiws/vol24/iss5/3.

22. A.L. Atchinson. "Where Are the Women? An Analysis of Gender Mainstreaming in Introductory Political Science Textbooks," https://doi.org/10.1080/15512169.2017.1279549.

23. I.L. Monforti, A. McGlynn. "*Aqui Estamos*? A Survey of Latino Portrayal in Introductory U.S. Government and Politics Textbooks," https://doi.org/10.1017/S1049096510000181.

24. S. Wood, J.A. Henning, L. Chen, T. McKibben, M.L. Smith, M. Weber, A. Zemenick, C.J. Ballen. "A Scientist Like Me: Demographic Analysis of Biology Textbooks Reveals Both Progress and Long-Term Lags," https://doi.org/10.1098/rsbp.2020.0877. Also see B. Brookshire. "College Biology Textbooks Still Portray a World of White Scientists," https://www.sciencenews.org/article/college-biology-textbooks-representation-white-men.

25. L. Norton, A. Palermo. "Breaking the Barriers—Towards a More Inclusive Chemical Sciences Community," https://doi.org/10.1515/pac-2021-0502.

26. C.L. Jarvis. "Chemistry Textbooks Still Lack Gender and Racial Representation," https://cen.acs.org/education/undergraduate-education/Chemistry-textbooks-still-lack-gender/99/i14.

27. M.L. Becker, M.R. Nilsson. "College Chemistry Textbooks Fail on Gender Representation," https://doi.org/10.1021/acs.jchemed.0c01037.

28. T.M. Lawler, T. Niiler. "Physics Textbooks from 1960–2016: A History of Gender and Racial Bias," https://doi.org/10.1119/1.55145525. Also see M. Hosseini, S. Sharifzad. "Gender Disparity in Publication Records: A Qualitative Study of Women Researchers in Computing and Engineering," https://doi.org/10.1186/s41073-021-00117-3.

29. L. McKenzie. "Tackling Racism in Textbook Publishing," https://www.insidehighered.com/news/2021/02/26/publisher-pearson-tries-tackle-systemic-rascism-higher-ed. Also see Pearson PLC. "Pearson Global Content and Editorial Policy," https://www.pearsonenespanol.com/PoliticalEditorial29092021.pdf. K. Forbes. "Feminist Organizing Around Gender Discrimination Lawsuits in Higher Education," https://doi.org/10.1353/ff.2018.0019.

30. A. Omeokwe. "CBO Projects Inflation, Economic Growth to Cool This year," https://www.wsj.com/articles/cbo-projects-inflation-economic-growth-to-cool-this year-next-11,653,501,643. Also see Congressional Budget Office. "The Budget and Economic Outlook: 2022–2032," https://www.cbo.gov/system/files/2022-05/579950-Outlook.pdf.

31. University of Michigan. "Surveys of Consumers," https://data.sca.isr.umich.edu/fetchdoc.php?docid=70222.

32. G. Ip. "On Inflation, Economics Has Some Explaining to Do," https://www.wsj.com/articles/on-inflation-economics-has-some-explaining-to-do-11655294432.

33. H. Torry, A. DeBarros. "Economists Say Recession Is Likely," *The Wall Street Journal,* June 21, 2022, p. A2.

34. B. Mena. "Consumer Sentiment at Record Low Is Another Ominous Sign for Economy," https://www.wsj.com/articles/consumer-sentiment-at-record-low-is-another-ominous-sign-for-economy-11656093116?mod=series_inflation. Also see C. Matthews. "Consumer Sentiment Hits New record Low, UMich Survey Finds," https://www.marketwatch.com/story/consumer-sentiment-remains-hits-new-record-low-umich-survey-finds-11656079555.

35. J. Mackintosh. "Larry Summers Nailed Inflation. But Is He Right on What Comes Next?" https://www.wsj.com/articles/larry-summers-nailed-inflation-but-is-he right-on-what-comes next-11,656,343,688?mod=hp_lead_pos13.

36. J. Cassidy. "Is Larry Summers Really Right About Inflation and Biden?" https://www.newyorker.com/news/our-columnists/is-larry-summers-really-right-about-inflation-and-biden.
37. R. Torchinsky. "Consumers' Economic Outlook Worsens," *The Wall Street Journal*, June 29, 2022, p. A2. Also see Federal Reserve Bank of Atlanta. "GDP Now," https://www.atlantafed.org/cqer/research/gdpnow.
38. J. Hilsenrath. "If the U.S. Is In a Recession, It's a Very Strange One," https://www.wsj.com/articles/recession-economy-unemployment-jobs-11656947596?mod=hp_lead_pos10.
39. B. Whitton. "Inflation Tracker: When Will Prices Stop Going Up?" https://www.wsj.com/articles/inflation-tracker-cpi-data-prices-11657717467?mod=rss_markets_main&mod=article_inli.
40. P. Hannan. "Global Economies Flash Warning of Sharp Slowdown," https://www.wsj.com/articles/global-economies-flash-warning-of-sharp-slowdown-11651247579?mod=hp_lead_pos1.
41. N. Timiraos. "Jerome Powell's Dilemma: What if the Drivers of Inflation Are Here to Stay? https://www.wsj.com/articles/inflation-jackson-hole-fed-powerr-11661288446?mod=hp-lead_pos5.
42. J. Milliot. "Higher Costs Dent Earnings Gains at HarperCollins," https://www.publishersweekly.com/pw/by-topic/industry-news/financial-reporting/article/88457-high-costs-dent-earnings-gains-at-harpercollins.html. N.B. *Publishers Weekly* also mentioned higher education in this and most of the following articles.
43. E. Nawotka. "Supply Squeeze, Changing Consumer Behavior Challenges Publishers," https://www.publishersweekly.com/pw/by-topic/industry-news//article/89251-supply-squeeeze-changing-consumer-behavior-challenges-publishers.html. J. Milliot. "A Wobbly Year for Print Book Sales," https://www.publishersweekly.com/pw/by-topic/industry-news/ bookselling/article/89397-a-wobbly-year-for-print-book-sales.html. J. Milliot. "Trade Publishing Flat in First Half of 2022," https:// www.publishersweekly.com/pw/by-topic/industry-news/financial-reporting/article/90112-trade-publishing-sales-flat-in-first-half-of 2022.html.
44. Barnes & Noble Education (BNED). "Barnes & Noble Education Reports Fourth Quarter and Fiscal Year 2022 Financial Results," https://www.businesswire.com/news/home/20220629005115/en/ Barnes-Noble-Education-Reports-Fourth-Quarter-and-Fiscal-Year-2022-Financial-Results. Also see J. Milliot. "Barnes & Noble Education Sees Improvement," https://www.publishersweekly.com/pw/by-topic/ industry-news/financial-reporting/article/89738-barnes-noble-education-sees-improvement.html. Barnes & Noble Education. "Barnes & Noble Education Reports First Quarter Fiscal year 2023 Financial Results,"

https://www.businesswire.com/news/home/20220831005126/
en/Barnes-Noble-Education-Reports-First-Quarter-Fiscal-Year-2023-
Financial-Results.National Association of College Stores (NACS).
"NACS Faculty Report: Use of Digital Course Materials Changes
as Campuses Reopen," https://www.nacs.org/nacs-faculty-report-
use-of-digital-course-materials-changes-as-campuses-reopen. Also see
National Association of College Stores (NACS). "NACS Report: Student
Spending on Course Materials Continues to Decline," https://www.
nacs.org/student-spending-on-course-materials-continues-to-decline.
PR Newswire. "College Students Still Prefer Print Despite Growing
eTextbook Popularity," https://www.prnewswire.com/news-releases/
college-students-still-prefer-print-despite-growing-etextbook-
populairty.301614822.html.

45. Global Data. "Pearson PLC," https://s3.amazonaws.com/attachment.
mergentassets.com/investext-full/single_116224859630a6d6a50a6c.
pdf. Also see Cengage. "Net Income to 4th Quarter 2022," https://www.
statista.com/statistics/801175/cengage-learning-higher-educayion-sales-
category. McGraw Hill. "Revenue of McGraw-Hill Education,"
file:///C:/Users,angre/Downloads/statistic_id800771_mcgraw-hill-
education-revenue-2013-2021.pdf. J. Milliot. "Wiley Sales Topped $2
Billion in Fiscal 2022," https://www.publishersweekly.com/pw/by-
topic/industry-news/financial-reporting/article/89628-wiley-sales-
topped-2-billion-in-fiscal-2022.html.

46. In the U.S., an academic semester is generally a 15-week term in the Fall
and a second in the Spring, a summer semester is generally optional.
Students in a traditional semester system generally take 4 or 5 courses each
semester, depending on the number of credits for each course. A quarter
semester system generally consists of 4 quarter semesters each 10 weeks
long offered in the Fall, Winter, Spring, and Summer semesters. Students
in a quarter semester system generally take 3 or 4 courses each quarter, and
this reduced academic load allows students to spend more time on a smaller
number of courses.

47. J. Salanga. "All Access" [at UC Davis], https://magazine.ucdavis.edu/
all-access. Also see UC Davis. "UC Davis: Building an Equitable Textbook
Subscription Service with VitalSource & Canvas," file:///C:/Users/
angre/Downloads/UC-Davis.pdf.

48. UC Davis Bookstores. "Equitable Access:," https://ucdavisstores.com/
EquitableAccess.

49. B. Rosenblatt. "UC Davis's Plan to Disrupt Textbook Publishing,"
https://copyrightandtechnology.com/201-/08/05/
uc-daviss-plan-to-disrupt-textbook-publishing.

50. C. Ruckman. "The Evolution of Inclusive Access," https://www.nacs.org/the-evolution-of-inclusive-accessedc9dbe2. Also see R. Anderson. "UC Davis Experiments with a New Textbook Model: An Interview with Jason Lorgan," https://scholarlykitchen.sspnet.org/2019/09/04/uc-davis-experiments-with-a-new-textbook-model-an-interview-with-jason-lorgan.

51. G. Blumenstyk. "Can a Health Insurance Model Bring 'Equitable Access' to the Textbook Market," https://www.chronicle.com/newsletter/the-edge/2019-06-18?cid2=gen_login_refresh&cid=gen_sign-in. Also see E. Olsen. "Flat-Fee Textbook Model at University of California, Davis," https://www.helixeducation.com/resources/blog/flat-fee-textbook-model-at-university-of-canifornia-davis. D. Lederman, S. Jaschik. "Textbooks, Affordability, and Equity of Access," https://www.inside-highered.com/sites/default/server_files/media/Slides%20Textbooks%20Affordability%20and%20Equity%20of%20Access.pdf.

52. Vital Source. UC Davis wanted a solution to the costs of college textbooks, and UC Davis asked VitalSource to build an Equitable Access system; https://get.vitalsource.com/vitalsource-advantage/equitable-access. Also see VitalSource. "Scaling an Equitable Access Program: VitalSource and University of California, Davis," https://www.get.vitabcource.com/vitalsource-advantage/equitable-access. VitalSource. "The Next Step in Course Materials Delivery from the Team You Trust and the Tools You Love," https://www.get.vitalsource.com/vitalsource-advantage/equitable-access.

53. R. Jansen. "10 Best Practices for an Equitable Access Program," https://www.ecampusnews.com/2022/05/31/top-10-best-practices-for-an-equitable-access-program.

54. E. Budnik. "Immediate Access Replaced With New Equitable Access Program for Textbooks," https://thedailyaztec.com/110142/news/immediate-access-replaced-with-new-equitable-access-program-for textbooks. Also see A.A. Smith. "Initiatives Underway for Low-Cost, Free Textbooks for California College Students," https://edsource.org/2019/low-cost-free-textbooks-for-california-college-students/616831. M. Burke. "Newsom's Bid to Make Textbooks Free Delayed in Community Colleges Central Office," https://edsource.org/2022/newsoms-bid-to-make-textbooks-free-delayed-in-community-colleges-central-office/675596.

55. Yogi Berra. "It's Tough to Make Predictions, Especially About the Future," https://www.goodreads.com/quotes/261863-it-s-tough-to-make-predictions-especially-about-the-future.

56. Heraclitus. "The only constant is change," https://socraticlife.com.au/heraclitus-the-only-constant-is-change.

57. F.S. Fitzgerald. *The Great Gatsby* (New York: Scribner, 2013), p. 192.

BIBLIOGRAPHY

D.A. Aaker. "Measuring Brand Equity Across Products and Markets." *California Management Review, 38*, 2 (1996), 102–120.

R. Agarwal, M. Gort. "First-Over Advantage and the Speed of Competitive Entry, 1887–1996." *Journal of Law and Economics, 44*, 1(April 2001),161–177.

N. Agate, C.E. Ball, A. Belan, M. McCormick, J. Nords-Fox. "Findable, Impactful, Citable, Usable, Sustainable: A Heuristic for Authors of Digital Publishing Projects, 2020." digitalcommons.wayne.edu/cgi/viewcontent.cgi?article=115 7&context=libsp.

P.G. Altbach. *The Knowledge Context: Comparative Perspectives on the Distribution of Knowledge* (Albany, NY: State University of New York Press, 1987).

P.G. Altbach, S. McVey. *Perspectives on Publishing* (Lexington, MA: Lexington Books, 1976).

S. Anderson, V. Ginsburgh. "Price Discrimination Via Second-Hand Markets. *European Economic Review, 38*, 1(1994), 23–44.

Association of American Publishers (AAP). "College course materials (Q &A): Frequently asked questions about student spending on course materials and inclusive access programs (2020)." poblishers.org/wp=content/ uploads/2020/05/Inclusive-Access-FAQ1.pdf.

Association of American Publishers. *The Higher Education Textbook Market: Prepared for Submission to the Advisory Committee on Student Financial Assistance* (New York: Association of American Publishers, 2006).

Association of American Publishers. *Higher Education Books and Materials. Annual Report* (New York: Association of American Publishers, 2009).

© The Author(s), under exclusive license to Springer Nature   115
Switzerland AG 2023
A. N. Greco, *The College Textbook Publishing Industry in the U.S. 2000-2022*, Marketing and Communication in Higher Education, https://doi.org/10.1007/978-3-031-30415-6

S. Athey, A. Schmutzler. "Investment and Market Dominance." *RAND Journal of Economics, 32*, 1(Spring 2001), 1–26.

Bain & Company. "Publishing in the Digital Era." www.bain.com/insights/publishing-in-the-digital-era.

D.C. Baker, J. Hileman. "Used Books and the College Textbook Industry." *Book Research Quarterly*, 33 (1987), 8–17.

Y. Bakos, E. Brynjolfsson. "Bundling and Competition on the Internet." *Marketing Science*, 19,1(2000), 63–82.

Y. Bakos, E. Brynjolfsson. "Bundling Information Goods: Pricing, Profits and Efficiency." *Management Science*, 45,12(1999), 1613–1630.

E.J. Balleisen. "The Prospects for Collaborative Research in Business History." *Enterprise & Society* 21,4(2020) 824–852.

J. Barzun. *On Writing, Editing, and Publishing* (Chicago, IL: University of Chicago Press, 1986).

S. Baum, J. Ma, *The College Board: Trends in College Pricing* (Washington, DC: College Board, 2007).

S. Bell. "Course Materials Adoption: A Faculty Survey and Outlook for the OER Landscape." www.choice360.org/content/2-librarianship/5-whitepaper/bell-white-paper-october-2018/100318_bell_white_paper.pdf.

S. Bell. "What About the Bookstore: Textbook Affordability Programs and the Academic Library-Bookstore Relationship?" Crin.acrl.org/index.php/crinewsissue/v.

V.M. Bennett, R. Seamans, F. Zhu. "Cannibalization and Option Value Effects of Secondary Markets: Evidence from the US Concert Industry." *Strategic Management Journal, 36* 11(2015), 1599–1614.

R. Benson-Amer, J. Sarakatsannis, K. Wee "The future of Textbooks." www.mckinsey.com/industries/social-sector/our-insights/the-future-of-textbooks.

G. Bittlingmayer. "The Elasticity of Demand for Books, Resale Price Maintenance and the Lerner Index." *Journal of Institutional and Theoretical Economics, 148*,4 (1992), 588–606.

J. Blumenthal. *The Printed Book in America* (Boston: D.R. Godine, 1977).

J. Boczar, L. Pascual. "E-Books for the Classroom and Open Access Textbooks: Two Ways to Help Students Save Money on Textbooks." *The Serials Librarian*, 72, 1–4(2017), https://doi.org/10.1080/0361526X.2017.1309830.

B. Bodo, D. Antal, A. Puha (2020). "Can Scholarly Pirate Libraries Bridge the Knowledge Access Gap? An Empirical Study on the Structural Conditions of Book Piracy in Global and European Academia." PlosONE. 15(12). e0242509. https://doi.org/10.1371/journal.pone.0242509.

A.M. Brandenburger, H.W. Stuart. "Value-Based Business Strategy, *Journal of Economics & Management Strategy, 5*,1(1996), 5–24.

V. J. Brenni. *Book Printing in Britain and America: A Guide to the Literature and a Directory of Printers* (Westport, CT: Greenwood Press, 1983).

E. Brynjolfsson, M.D. Smith. "Frictionless Commerce? A Comparison of Internet and Conventional Retailers." *Management Science, 46*,4(April 2000a), 563–585.

E. Brynjolfsson, M.D. Smith. "The Great equalizer? Consumer Choice Behavior at Internet Shopbots." Working Paper MIT Sloan School of Management (July 2000b), 1–63.

J. Bulow. "Durable-Goods Monopolists." *Journal of Political Economy, 90*, 2(1982), 314–332.

J. Bulow. "An Economic Theory of Planned Obsolescence." *Quarterly Journal of Economics, 101*,4(1986), 729–749.

R.G. Calkins. *Illuminated Books of the Middle Ages* (Ithaca, NY: Cornell University Press, 1983).

B. Carbaugh. "College Textbook Publishing: Three Microeconomic Applications." *The American Economist 61*, 2(2016), 191–202.

A. Capaccioni. "Origins and Developments of the Open Access Books." www.intechopen.com/online-first/origins-and-developments-of-the-open-access-books.

S. Casper. "Textbooks Today and Tomorrow: A Conversation About History, Pedagogy, and Economics." *Journal of American History,* 100, 4(March 2014), 1139–1169.

O. Chatain. "Value Creation, Competition, and Performance in Buyer-Supplier Relationships." *Strategic Management Journal, 32*,1(2011), 76–102.

J. Chen, S. Esteban, M. Shum. "When Do Secondary Markets Harm Firms?" *American Economic Review, 103*,7(2013), 2911–2934. 30.

L. Chen. "Retailers' Differentiation Strategy and Pricing in the Retail Market of Digital Content: A case of E-Textbooks." *Journal of Theoretical and Applied Electronic Commerce, Research* 14, 3(2019), 61–76.

K. Clay, K. Ramayya, E. Wolf. "Prices and Price Dispersion on the Web: Evidence From the Online Book Industry." *Journal of Industrial Economics, 49*, 4(December 2001), 521–539.

S.K. Clerides. "Pricing, Product Selection, and Consumer Choice in a Durable Good Market: The Book Publishing Industry." Ph. D. dissertation (1998), Yale University.

J.Y. Cole (ed.). *Books in Our Future: Perspectives and Proposals* (Washington, DC: Library of Congress/Center for the Book, 1987).

College Board. "Trends in College Pricing." www.collegeboard.com/prod_downloads/press/cost03/cb_trends_pricing_2003.pdf.

E. Costello, R. Bolger. "Textbook Authors, Publishers, Formats, and Costs in Higher." *BMC Res Notes (2019),* https://doi.org/10.1186/s13104-019-4099-1.

P. Crosby. "Don't Judge a Book by Its Cover: Examining Digital Disruption in the Book Industry Using a Stated-Preference Approach." *Journal of Cultural Economics.* https://doi.org/10.1007/s10824-019-09363-2.

W.M. Cross, M. Waller. "Prototyping the Open Textbook Toolkit: Digital Infrastructure that Connects Libraries, Disciplinary Faculty, and University Presses to Support Open Education." digital.sandiego.edu/symposium/2017/2017/12.

P.A. Curry. "Uncertainty and the Decision Making Under Uncertainty and the Evolution of Independent Preferences." *Journal of Economic Theory, 98,* 2(June 2001), 357–369.

T.H. Davenport, J.G.T. Harris. "What People Want (And How to Predict It)." *MIT Sloan Management Review, 50,* 2(2009), 22.

L.M. Davis, M. Usry. "Faculty Selling Desk Copies—The Textbook Industry, the Law, and the Ethics." *Journal of Academic Ethics,* 9, 1(2011), 19–31.

A. De Vany, D. Walls. "Bose-Einstein Dynamics and Adaptive Contracting in the Motion Picture Industry." *The Economic Journal, 106,439(November 1996),* 1493–1514.

D.F. DiClemente, D. A. Hantula. "Applied Behavioral Economics and Consumer Choice." *Journal of Economic Psychology, 24,* 5(October 2003), 589–602.

E.M. Dinlersoz, L. Han. "The Shipping Strategies of Internet Retailers: Evidence From Internet Book Retailing." *Quantitative Marketing and Economics, 4,* 4(2006), 407–438.

P. Drucker. *Management: Tasks, Responsibilities, Practices* (New York: Harper & Row, 1984).

E.L. Eisenstein. *The Printing Press as an Agent of Change, 2 Vols.* (New York: Cambridge University Press, 1979).

M. Fairchild. "Rip-Off 101: How the Current Practices of Textbook Industry Drive Up the Cost of College Textbook." CALPIRG Higher Education Project, www.maketextbooksaffordable.org/ripoff101.pdf.

R. Farrington. "How to Combat the Rising Cost of College Textbooks, www.forbes.com/sites/robert/farrington/2019/08/22/how-to-combat-the-rising-cost-of-college-textbooks/#402d19f7798b.

C.L. Ferguson. "Textbooks in Academic Libraries." *Serials Review,* 42, 3(2016), 252–258.

Foster, J.E., A.W. Horowitz. "Complimentarily Yours: Free Examination Copies and Textbook Prices." *International Journal of Industrial Organization, 14,* 1(1996), 85–99.

B.E. Foucault, D.A. Scheufel. "Web vs. Campus Store? Why Students Buy Textbooks Online." *Journal of Consumer Marketing, 19,* 4/5(2002), 409–423.

J. Fox. "College Students Catch a Break on One Cost At Least." www.bloomberg.com/opinion/articles/2020-02-08/collete-textbook-prices-plateau-with-rentals-and-digital-option.

L. Gaston, B. Williams. "In Search of a Low-Cost Textbook." *Southern Business Review,* 35, 2(2010), 41–44.

A. Ghose, M.D. Smith, R. Telang. "Internet Exchanges for Used Books: An Empirical Analysis of Welfare Implications." New York University, Stern School of Business Working Paper (2005).

A. Graha. "The Assessment: Economics of the Internet." *Oxford Review of Economic Policy*, 17, 2(2001), 145–158.

A.N. Greco. "The Impact of Horizontal Mergers and Acquisitions on Corporate Concentration in the U.S. Book Publishing Industry, 1989–1994." *The Journal of Media Economics*, 12, 3(Fall 1999), 165–180.

A.N. Greco. "Mergers and Acquisitions in Publishing, 1984–1988: Some public policy issues." *Book Research Quarterly*, 5, 4(Fall 1989), 25–44.

A.N. Greco, C.E. Rodriguez, R.M. Wharton. *Culture and Commerce of Publishing in the 21st Century* (Stanford, CA: Stanford University Press, 2007).

S. Handler. "McGraw Hill, Others Allege 'Massive' Textbook Counterfeiting." news.bloomberglaw.com/ip-law/mcgraw-hill-others-allege-massive-textbook-counterfeiting.

I. Hendel, A. Lizzeril. "Interfering with Secondary Markets." *RAND Journal of Economics*, 30, 1(1999), 1–21.

M. Horvitz. "The Pricing of Textbooks and the Remuneration of Authors. *American Economic Review*, 56, 1/2(1966), 412–420.

T. Iizuka. "An Empirical Analysis of Planned Obsolescence." *Journal of Economics & Management Strategy*, 16, 1(2007), 191–226.

International Monetary Fund. "World Economic Outlook: A Long and Difficult Ascent." www.elibrary.imf.org/doc/IMF081/29296-9781513556055/29296-9781513556055/Other_formats/Source_PDF/292963-9781513558158.pdf.

A. Johns. *Piracy: The Intellectual Property Wars from Gutenberg to Gates* (Chicago: University of Chicago Press, 2009).

B. Klein, A.V. Lerner, K. Murphy. "The Economics of Copyright 'Fair Use' in a Networked World." *The American Economic Review*, 92, 2(May 2002), 205–208.

J.A. Lambert, J. Ojala, J.P. Gustafsson. "Strategy and Business History Rejoined: How and Why Strategic Management Concepts Took Over Business History." www.tandfonline.com/doi/pdf/10.1080/00076791.2020.1856076.

K. Lee, K. Han, B. Lee. "Impact of Digital Distribution in the Publishing Market: A Synthetic Content Approach." Papers.ssrn.com/sol3/papers/cfm/abstract_id=3559782.

A. Lierman. "Textbook Alternative Incentive Programs at U.S. Universities: A Review of the Literature." C:/Users/angre/Downloads/29758-Article%20Text-83270-1-10-20201212%20(1).pdf.

Library Journal. "Academic Faculty: Textbook & Course Materials Affordability Survey Report." www.s3.amazonaws.com/WebVault/research/Academic%20Faculty%20Course%20Materials%20Study%20REPORT-FINAL.pdf.

J. Manza, M. Sauder, N. Wright. "Pricing Textbook, Sociology." *European Journal of Sociology*, 51, 2(2010), 271–304.

N. Maron, R. Kennison. "Open and Equitable Scholarly Communications: Creating a More Inclusive Future." www.ala.org/acrl/sites/ala.org.acri/files/content/publications/booksanddigitalresources/digital.resec.pdf.

L. McKenna. "Why Students Are Still Spending So Much for College Textbooks." www.theatlantic.com/education/archive/2018/01/why-students=are-still-spending-so-much-for-college-textbooks/551639.

L. Meredith, D. Maki. "Product Cannibalization and the Role of Prices." *Applied Economics, 33,* 14(2000), 1785–1793.

J. Milbum. "The Relationship Between Fair Value, Market Value, and Efficient Markets." *Accounting Perspectives, 7,* 4(2008), 293.

A.R. Miller, M.H. Davis. *Intellectual Property: Patents, Trademarks, and Copyright* (St. Paul, MN: West Wadsworth, 2000).

J.R. Miller, A.W. Nutting, L. Baker-Eveleth. "The Determinants of Electronic Textbook Use Among College Students." *The American Economist, 68,* 1(2013), 41–50.

L. Miller. "On Killing Off the Market for Used Textbooks and the Relationship Between Markets for New and Secondhand Goods." *Journal of Political Economy, 82,* 3(1974), 612–619.

J. Mitchell. "A Tough Lesson for College Textbook Publishers." www.wsj.com/articles/a-tough-lesson-for-college-textbook-publishers-1409182139.

K. Molina. "Digital Asset Pricing in the Textbook Market." ssrn.com/abstract=1868262.

J. Moro. "The Emergence of Digital Course Materials in Higher Education and their Effectiveness in Teaching and Engaging Students." *Publishing Research Quarterly*, 34, 3(September 2018), 417–429.

M. Morris-Babb, S. Henderson. "An Experiment in Open-Access Textbook Publishing: Changing the World One Textbook at a Time." *Journal of Scholarly Publishing, 43,* 2(2012), 148–155.

C. Nagle, K. Vietz "Fixing the Broken Textbook Market, 2nd ed." uspirg.org/sites/pirg/files/report/Fixing%20the%20broken%20Textbook%20Market%20June%202020_0.pdf.

K.T. Nevena, P.K. Kannan, B.T. Ratchford. "Product Form Bundling: The Implications for Marketing Digital Products." *Journal of Retailing, 84,* 2(2008). 181.

A. Nevo. "A Practitioner's Guide to Estimation of Random-Coefficients Logit Models of Demand." *Journal of Economics & Management Strategy, 9,* 4(2000), 513–548.

C. Newport. "Why Are So Many Knowledge Workers Quitting? The Coronavirus Threw Everyone into Walden Pond." www.newyorker.com/culture/office-space/why-are-so-many-knowledge-workers-quitting.

N.H. Nicholls. "Demographic Data on Textbooks and Usage Statistics: Implications for Textbook Cost-Saving Analysis." apps.lob.umich.edu/files/Cost-Analysis-Student-Survey.pdf.

Y. Odin, N. Odin, P. Valette-Florence. "Conceptual and Operational Aspects of Brand Loyalty: An Empirical Investigation." *Journal of Business Research, 53,* 2(2001), 75–84.

N. Oraiopoulos, M.E. Ferguson, L.B. Toktay. "Relicensing as a Secondary Market Strategy." *Management Science, 58,* 5(2012), 1022–1037.

M. Parry. "Students Get Savvier About Textbook Buying." www.chronicle.com/article/Students-Get=Savvier-About/136827.

B.K. Pathak. "Development of a Markov Decision Process-Based Model for Controlling Secondary Market Sales: The Example of the Online Market for Used Textbooks." *International Journal of Management, 27,* 3(2010), 704–712, 777.

S. Paxiha. "The Challenges of Higher Education Digital Publishing." *Publishing Research Quarterly, 27,* 4(2011), *321–326.*

L. J. Peet. "Textbook Affordability Survey: Costs Still a Concern, OER An Opportunity." www.libraryjournal.com/?detailStory=Lj=textbook=affordability-survey-costs-still-a-c0ncern-oer-an-opportunity.

J.H. Politz, A. Christie. "The High Cost of Textbooks: A Convergence of Academic Libraries, Campus Bookstores, Publishers." Digitalcommons.unl.edu/ejasljournal/69.

M.E. Porter. *Competitive Strategy: Techniques for Analyzing Industries and Competitors* (New York: Free Press, 1980).

M.E. Porter. Towards a Dynamic Theory of Strategy. *Strategic Management Journal 12(1991):* 95–117.

M.E. Porter, S. Stern. "Innovation: Location Matters." MIT Sloan Management Review 42(2001), 4, 28–36.

R. Poynder. "Open Access: 'Information Wants to Be Free'? digitalcommons.unl.edu/cgi/viewcontent.cgi?article=1184&context=scholcom.

K. Raustiala, C. Sprigman. "The Piracy Paradox Revisited." *Stanford Law Review, 61,*5(2009), 6–11.

R. Reynolds. "Trends Influencing the Growth of Digital Textbooks in U.S. Higher Education." *Publishing Research Quarterly, 27,* 2(2011), 178–187.

T. Ross-Hellaer, B. Fecher, K. Shearer, E.L. Rodrigues. "Pubfair: A Framework for Sustainable, Distributed, Open Science Publishing Services, Comments." coar-wp-content/uploads/2019/09/Pubfair_A-framework-for-sustainable-distributed-open-sciencepublishing=services.pdf.

H.J. Rotfeld and T. Clark. "The Textbook Effect: Conventional Wisdom, Myth, and Error in Marketing," *Journal of Marketing 64,* 2(April 2000), 122–126.

R. Rust. "When Is It Optimal to Kill Off the Market for Used Durable Goods?" *Econometrica, 54,* 1(1986), 65–86. 31.

M. Schmitt, T. Shi. "Secondary Markets and Firm Profits: Evidence from College Textbooks." www.anderson.ucla.edu/Documents/areas/fac/policy/SchmiyyShi_SecondaryMarkets_09102018.pdf.

J.E. Seaman, J. Seaman. "Inflection Point: Educational Resources in U.S. Higher Education." www.bayviewanalytics.com/reports/2019inflectionpoint.pdf.

J.E. Seaman, J. Seaman. "Turning Point for Digital Curricula: Educational Resources in U.S. Higher Education, 2022," https://www.bayviewanalytics.com/reports/turningpointdigitalcurricula.pdf.

E. Senack. "Fixing the Broken Textbook Market: How Students Respond to High Textbook Costs and Demand Alternatives." uspirg.org/reports/usp/fixing-broken-textbook-market.

S. Shavell, T. van Ypersele. "Rewards Versus Intellectual Property Rights." *Journal of Law and Economics, 44*, 2(2001), 525–547.

J. Shelstad. "How Flat World Knowledge is Transforming College Textbook Publishing." *Publishing Research Quarterly, 27*, 3(2011), 254–258.

B.R. Shiller. "Digital Distribution and the Prohibition of Resale Markets for Information Goods." *Quantitative Marketing and Economics, 11*, 4(2013), 403–435.

R.J. Shiller. "Conversation, Information, and Herd Behavior." *Rhetoric and Human Behavior, 85*, 2(1995), 181–185.

R.J. Shiller. *Irrational Exuberance* (Princeton: Princeton University Press, 2000).

L.S. Silver, R.E. Tiger, K.E. Clow. "Quantitative Methods Professors' Perspectives on the Cost of College Textbooks." *Academy of Information and Management Sciences, 14*, 2(2011), 39–55.

G.V. Smith, R.L. Parr. *Valuation of Intellectual Property and Intangible Assets, 3rd ed.* (New York: John Wiley & Sons, 2000).

M.D. Smith, E. Brynjolfsson. "Consumer Decision-Making at an Internet Shopbot: Brand Still Matters." *The Journal of Industrial Economics, XLIX*, 4(December 2001), 541–558.

M.D. Smith, H. Nasir, J. Chang, S. Pasala, S.C. Lai, Y.W. Ng. "Analysis of Economic Impact of New Online Book Content Delivery Models on Traditional Online Book Retailers." Carnegie Mellon University, Tepper School of Business; H. John Heinz III School of Public Policy and Management Working Paper (2010).

A.M. Snowman. "Do Textbooks Have a Place in the Library?" *Journal of Access Management, 14*, 2(2017), doi.org/10.1080/15367967.2017.1309246.

D. Snyder. "120 years of American Education: A Statistical Portrait." www.nces.ed.gov/pubs93/93442.pdf.

F. Spence. "Consumer Experience and the Value of Search in the Online Textbook Market." www.law.northwestern.edu/research-faculty/cibe/events/internet/documents/Spence_ExperiemceAndSearch.pdf.

K. Stanberry. "The Changing World of International Protection of Intellectual Property." *Publishing Research Quarterly*, 7, 2(Spring 1991), 61–78.

S.H. Steinberg. *Five Hundred Years of Printing* (New York: Penguin, 1994).

J.E. Stiglitz. "The Contributions of the Economics of Information to Twentieth Century Economics." *Quarterly Journal of Economics, 115,* 4(November 2000), 1441–1478.

J.E. Stiglitz. "Economic Textbooks: Innovation and Product Differentiation." *Journal of Economic Education,* 19, 2(1988): 171–177.

J.E. Stiglitz. *Globalization and its Discontents* (New York: W.W. Norton, 2002).

W.S. Strong. *The Copyright Book: A Practical Guide, 5th ed.* (Cambridge, MA: M. I. T. Press, 1999).

W.N.A.W. Sulaiman, S.E. Mustafa. "Theory on Exploring Acceptance and Adoption of Digital Textbooks: A Guide for the Book Publishing Industry." *Publishing Research Quarterly,* 36, 3(September 2020), 381–398.

P.L. Swan. "Durability of Consumption Goods." *American Economic Review, 60,* 5(1970), 884–894.

M. Szenberg, L.E. Youngkoo. "The Structure of the American Book Publishing Industry." *Journal of Cultural Economics, 18,* 4(December 1994), 313–322.

J.A. Talaga, L.A. Tucci. "Consumer Tradeoffs in On-Line Textbook Purchasing." *Journal of Consumer Marketing,* 18, 1(2001), 10–20.

J.A. Talaga. "Forecasting Methods and Practices of Academic Textbook Publishers." *Book Research Quarterly,* 5, 4(1989), 58–67.

J. Tebbel. *Between Covers: The Rise and Transformation of Book Publishing in America* (New York: Oxford University Press, 1987).

J. Tebbel. *A History of Book Publishing in the United States, Vol. 4, The Great Change, 1940–1980* (New York: R.R. Bowker, 1981).

L.A. Thomas. "Incumbent Firms' Response to Entry: Price, Advertising, and New Product Introduction." *International Journal of Industrial Organization,* 17, 4(May 1999), 527–555.

P.H. Thornton. "Institutional Logics and the Historical Contingency of Power in Organizations: Executive Succession in the Higher Education Publishing Industry." *The American Journal of Sociology, 105,* 3(November 1999), 801–843.

P.H. Thornton. "Personal Versus Market Logics of Control: A Historically Contingent Theory of the Risk of Acquisition." *Organization Science, 72,* 3(May-June 2001), 294–311.

University of Michigan Office of the Provost. "Textbook Task Force Report: Research and Recommendations Concerning the Costs of Textbooks." Ann Arbor, MI: UM Office of the Provost (2007). www.provost.umich.edu/reports/Textbook_Task_Force_Final_Report.pdf.

U.S. Department of Education, Office of Educational Research and Improvement. *120 Years of American Education: A Statistical Portrait* (Washington D.C., U.S. Government Printing Office, 1993).

U.S. Government Accountability Office. "College Textbooks: Students Have Greater Access to Textbook Information." www.gao.gov/products/GAO-13-368.

M. Waldman. "A New Perspective on Planned Obsolescence." *Quarterly Journal of Economics, 108,* 1(1993), 273–283.

M.G. Watt. "Research on the Textbook Publishing Industry in the United States of America." files.eric.ed.gov/fulltext/ED498713.pdf.

J.T. Winterich. *Early American Books and Printing* (Boston and New York: Houghton Mifflin Company, Riverside Press, 1935)

M. Weisberg. "Student Attitudes and Behaviors Towards Digital Textbooks." *Publishing Research Quarterly, 27,* 2(2011), 188–196.

P. Whitten. "College Textbook Publishing in the 1970s." *The Annals of the American Academy of Political and Social Sciences, 421(1975),* 56–66.

T. Wu "How Professors Help Rip Off Students." www.nytimes.com/2019/12/11/opinion/textbook-prices-college.html.

R.J. Zboray. *A Fictive People: Antebellum Economic Development and the American Reading Public* (New York: Oxford University Press, 1993).

B.A. Zinser, G.L. Brunswick, I.A. Zaenglein. "The Ethical Implications of Publisher's Accelerated Revisions to Introductory Business Textbooks." *Academy of Marketing Studies, 17,*1(2013), 51–59.

INDEX

© The Author(s), under exclusive license to Springer Nature Switzerland AG 2023
A. N. Greco, *The College Textbook Publishing Industry in the U.S. 2000-2022*, Marketing and Communication in Higher Education, https://doi.org/10.1007/978-3-031-30415-6

The manufacturer's authorised representative in the EU is Springer
Nature Customer Service Centre GmbH, Europaplatz 3, 69115 Heidelberg,
Germany. If you have any concerns regarding our products, please
contact ProductSafety@springernature.com

Printed and bound by CPI Group (UK) Ltd, Croydon, CR0 4YY

29/04/2026
02099525-0006